William Edward Addis

**Christianity and the Roman Empire**

William Edward Addis

**Christianity and the Roman Empire**

ISBN/EAN: 9783337244538

Printed in Europe, USA, Canada, Australia, Japan

Cover: Foto ©Lupo / pixelio.de

More available books at **www.hansebooks.com**

*MANUALS OF EARLY CHRISTIAN HISTORY*
EDITED BY J. ESTLIN CARPENTER, M.A.

# CHRISTIANITY
## AND THE
# ROMAN EMPIRE

BY

W. E. ADDIS, M.A.
(Of Balliol College, Oxford)

London
THE SUNDAY SCHOOL ASSOCIATION
ESSEX HALL, ESSEX STREET, STRAND, W.C.
1898

# PREFATORY NOTE

THE early history of Christianity cannot be uninteresting to those who wish to be counted among the disciples of Jesus. During the first three hundred years of its existence, the tendencies which afterwards marked the great Churches of Christendom, began clearly to display themselves. And even within this short period the complex movement to which we give the name of Christianity, may be treated from several different points of view. It may be regarded as the manifestation of a great moral and religious impulse, and the stress will then fall on its power of quickening the inner forces of character, and transforming the whole standard of feeling and action. It may be conceived in its theological aspect, as a doctrine concerning God, Christ, and man, and the significance of its development will then lie in the successive forms through which the Christian faith was expressed, the circumstances which influenced them, and the intellectual and spiritual needs which they satisfied. Or again, it may be understood as embodied in the great institution known as the Church, through which the believer was admitted to the mystic fellowship of a divine life. Under this aspect the history of Christianity is the history of its institutions, and the ideas which animated them, its orders, its sacraments, its discipline, its worship and usage.

Along each of these lines the cause of Christianity was affected at every step by the conditions amid which it had to make its way. The single phrase 'the Roman Empire' sums up an immense number of elements, political, social, intellectual, moral, which immediately began to influence it, as soon as it travelled with the Apostle Paul beyond the limits of Syria, and sought to address the Gentile as well as the Jew. It is the object of this book to describe these influences, and to sketch their effect upon the general growth of the Church. Successive volumes will deal, it is hoped, with Christian morals, Christian doctrine, and Christian institutions.

It is not possible to discuss so intricate a subject without assuming some knowledge on the part of the reader. But it is believed that a very elementary acquaintance with the familiar facts of general history will make this little work intelligible. For the sake of those who may desire some introduction to the early Christian writers, but may only have access to translations such as are contained in the Ante-Nicene Christian Library, the chief works are cited by their English titles. In the Appendices an attempt has been made to supply such information concerning the principal persons whose names appear in these pages, as will enable the reader to refer them without difficulty to their proper date, locality, and school of thought.

J. E. C.

February, 1893.

# TABLE OF CONTENTS.

## CHAPTER I.

### THE ROMAN EMPIRE.

|  | PAGE. |
|---|---|
| The Assistance given by the Roman Empire to Christianity | 1 |
| § 1. The Geographical Limits of the Empire | 3 |
| § 2. The Unity of the Empire | 5 |
| (1) Unity of Government secured by Imperial Rule | 5 |
| (2) The Emperor and the Roman Senate | 6 |
| (3) The Roman Peace | 8 |
| (4) The Unity of Law | 9 |
| (5) Unity promoted by Fusion of Language and Race | 11 |
| § 3. The Influence of Religion | 12 |
| (1) Vitality of Religion | 12 |
| (a) Decline among the Educated | 13 |
| (b) Revival of the Ancient Religions | 13 |
| (c) Universal Belief in the Marvellous | 14 |
| (d) Witness of Sceptical Writers to the Supernatural | 14 |
| (2) Developments of the Old Roman Religion | 15 |
| (3) Blending of New Worships | 16 |
| (4) Their Deeper Moral Significance | 17 |
| (5) Religious Associations | 18 |

TABLE OF CONTENTS vii.
PAGE.
§ 4. Influence of Philosophy . . . . . . 20
   (1) Philosophers as Teachers and Preachers . 20
   (2) Their Practical Aims . . . . . 21
   (3) Stoicism. . . . . . . . 21
      (a) Its Earlier Form in Greece . . . 21
      (b) How modified when transplanted to Rome 22
      (c) Its Humanity. . . . . . 24
   (4) Platonism, as represented by Plutarch . . 25
   (5) Neo-Platonism . . . . . . 26
§ 5. Summary of Results . . . . . . 28

## CHAPTER II.

### THE CHRISTIAN MISSION.

§ 1. Why the Christian Mission travelled Westwards . 29
   (1) The Empire lay West of Palestine . . 29
   (2) The Jews had prepared the Way . . . 30
§ 2. The Jews in the Dispersion . . . . . 31
   (1) Their Social State . . . . . . 31
   (2) Their Legal Position . . . . . 32
   (3) Jewish Proselytes . . . . . . 33
§ 3. The Spread of Christianity during the First Century 35
   (1) Jerusalem and Antioch . . . . . 35
   (2) The New Name . . . . . . 36
   (3) St. Paul, St. Peter, and St. John . . . 37
   (4) The Apostolic Age . . . . . 38
§ 4. Advance in the next two Centuries . . . . 41
   (1) In the East . . . . . . . 41
   (2) Asia Minor . . . . . . . 43
   (3) Greece . . . . . . 44
   (4) Egypt . . . . . . . . 44
   (5) Rome and Italy . . . . . . 44
   (6) Africa . . . . . . . . 45
   (7) Gaul . . . . . . . . 46
   (8) Spain, Germany, Britain . . . . 47
§ 5. How Churches began . . . . . . 49
§ 6. Numbers of the Christians . . . . . . 50

## CHAPTER III.

### THE LEGAL POSITION OF CHRISTIANITY: THE PERSECUTIONS.

|  | PAGE. |
|---|---|
| § 1. General Antipathy to the Christian Religion | 53 |
|    (1) In what sense Polytheism is tolerant | 54 |
|    (2) The Charge of Atheism | 55 |
|    (3) Secrecy of Christian Assemblies | 56 |
|    (4) Contempt of the Educated | 57 |
| § 2. Christianity Illegal | 58 |
|    (1) As a new Religion, and a System of Magic | 58 |
|    (2) As Sacrilegious and Treasonable | 59 |
|    (3) As contravening the Law against Clubs | 59 |
| § 3. Varying Rigour of the Magistrates | 60 |
|    (1) The Emperors and Christianity | 61 |
|    (2) Peculiarity of the Christian Position | 62 |
| § 4. The Three Periods of Persecution | 63 |
| § 5. The First Period | 64 |
|    (1) The Christians hardly distinguished from the Jews | 64 |
|    (2) Nero: A.D. 64 | 66 |
|    (3) Local and Accidental Character of the Persecution | 67 |
|    (4) Domitian and Nerva, A.D. 81-96, 96-98 | 68 |
| § 6. The Second Period | 69 |
|    (1) Pliny's Report and Trajan's Answer, A.D. 112 | 69 |
|       (a) Pliny in Bithynia | 69 |
|       (b) Trajan's Rescript | 70 |
|       (c) Significance of his Policy | 71 |
|    (2) Hadrian, A.D. 117-138 | 71 |
|    (3) Martyrdoms under Antoninus Pius, A.D. 138-161 | 72 |
|    (4) Marcus Aurelius, A.D. 161-180 | 73 |
|       (a) His Reasons for Persecution | 73 |
|       (b) Altered Policy under Commodus, A.D. 180-193 | 74 |

## TABLE OF CONTENTS

§ 6. The Second Period (*continued*)—
- (5) Changed Political System . . . . 75
  - (*a*) Septimius Severus began a Military Despotism, A.D. 193-211 . . . 75
  - (*b*) His Treatment of the Christians . . 76
- (6) Friendly Feeling of Emperors of Eastern Origin 77
  - (*a*) Blending of Religions under Elagabalus, A.D. 218-222 . . . . 77
  - (*b*) Alexander Severus, A.D. 222-235 . 78

§ 7. The Third Period . . . . . . . 79
- (1) Decius, A.D. 249-251 . . . . . 80
  - (*a*) His Increased Severity . . . 80
  - (*b*) Political Reasons for conflict with Christians . . . . . 80
- (2) Effects on the Christians . . . . 81
- (3) The Successors of Decius . . . . 82
- (4) Forty Years of Peace . . . . . 84
- (5) The Last Effort to stamp out Christianity . 85
  - (*a*) Diocletian, A.D. 284 . . . . 85
  - (*b*) Galerius, and the Division of the Administration . . . . 86
- (6) Beginning of the Persecution, A.D. 303 . . 87
- (7) Its Duration and Extent . . . . 89
  - (*a*) With the Abdication of Diocletian, A.D. 305, the Unity of the Empire ceased . . . . . . 89
  - (*b*) Consequent Variations in the Intensity of the Persecution . . . . 89
- (8) The Edicts of Toleration . . . . 90

§ 8. The Peace of the Church . . . . . . 91

## CHAPTER IV.

### THE LEARNED DEFENCE OF CHRISTIANITY.

§ 1. Changes in the Second Century . . . . . 93
- (1) Growth of External Unity . . . . 94
- (2) Contrast with the Spontaneous Unity of the Early Church . . . . . . 95

## TABLE OF CONTENTS

|  | PAGE. |
|---|---|
| § 2. Influence of Greek Converts | 96 |
|   (1) Fruitfulness of Greek Ideas | 96 |
|   (2) Translation into Terms of Greek Thought | 97 |
|     (*a*) The Questions of Educated Converts | 97 |
|     (*b*) The Search for Theory and System | 98 |
|   (3) The Passage from Speculation to Orthodoxy | 98 |
| § 3. Philosophic Treatment of Judaism | 99 |
|   (1) Philo expounds the Old Testament with the Help of Greek Thought | 99 |
|   (2) His Need of a Doctrine of the Origin of the World | 101 |
|     (*a*) The Ancient Hebrews did not discuss Philosophical Questions | 101 |
|     (*b*) The 'Words' of God in Nature | 101 |
|     (*c*) The Corruptible and the Incorruptible Life | 103 |
|   (3) The System of Allegorical Interpretation | 103 |
| § 4. The Apologists as Christian Philosophers | 105 |
|   (1) Need of Justifying Christianity to the Jews | 105 |
|   (2) Changed Reasoning in addressing the Greeks | 106 |
|   (3) The First Apologists and Philosophy | 107 |
| § 5. The Chief Apologists | 108 |
|   (1) Justin the Martyr | 109 |
|   (2) Tatian; Athenagoras; Minucius Felix | 110 |
| § 6. Their Attitude to Judaism | 111 |
|   (1) Treatment of the Law | 112 |
|   (2) They brought Revelation to confirm the Conclusions of Philosophy | 113 |
| § 7. Justin and the Doctrine of the Logos | 114 |
|   (1) The Logos enlightened Greeks and Hebrews | 114 |
|     (*a*) Born into Personal Existence; identified with Christ | 114 |
|     (*b*) The Organ of Revelation from the Beginning | 115 |
|   (2) Advantages of Christianity as a Revealed Religion | 116 |
|   (3) The Greeks derived Wisdom from the Jewish Scriptures | 117 |

## TABLE OF CONTENTS

§ 7. Justin and the Doctrine of the Logos (*continued*)—
- (4) How Justin mingled Philosophy with Religion ... 119
- (5) The Attitude of the other Apologists to Greek Philosophy ... 120
- (6) And to Revelation ... 121

§ 8. Preparation for a Dogmatic System ... 122
- (1) The Apologists were the Fathers of Theology ... 122
- (2) Their View of Christian Dogmas ... 123
- (3) The Dogmatic System still in the Germ ... 124
  - (*a*) Subsequent Restriction of the Scope of Philosophy ... 124
  - (*b*) The Apologists erected no Articles of Faith ... 125
  - (*c*) Their Theology Heretical when judged by Later Standards ... 125

## CHAPTER V.
### CHANGED ASPECTS OF CHRISTIANITY.

§ 1. Twofold Unity of Creed and Organisation ... 127

§ 2. Altered Relations to Judaism ... 129
- (1) Debt of the Catholic to the Jewish Church ... 129
- (2) Distinction between the Moral and the Ceremonial Law ... 130
  - (*a*) Why the Controversy about the Law died away ... 130
  - (*b*) Permanent Value of its Rules of Morality ... 131
- (3) Contrast with the Position of St. Paul ... 132

§ 3. New Prominence of Morality ... 133
- (1) Morality and Religion: Jesus and Epictetus ... 134
- (2) The New Law: Salvation by Works ... 135
- (3) Ascetical Character of Christian Morality ... 136
- (4) Views of Marriage ... 137
- (5) Consequent Dangers ... 139

§ 4. Decay of the Expectation of Christ's Second Coming ... 140
- (1) The Belief among the Early Christians ... 140
- (2) Declines under the Influence of the Greek Spirit ... 142

## CHAPTER VI.

### THE ATTEMPT TO MAKE CHRISTIANITY AN INTELLECTUAL SYSTEM.

|  | PAGE. |
|---|---|
| § 1. Dangers arising from Contact with Greek Thought | 144 |
|    (1) Tendencies to Divisions and Sects. | 144 |
|    (2) How Counteracted by the Rise of the Catholic Church | 146 |
| § 2. The Extreme Intellectualism of the Gnostics | 147 |
|    (1) The Eastern Gnostics: Simon the Samaritan Magician | 147 |
|    (2) The Alexandrian Gnostics | 148 |
|    (3) The Gnostics compared with the Apologists. | 149 |
| § 3. General Characteristics of Gnosticism | 150 |
|    (1) Based on the Opposition of Matter and Spirit | 151 |
|    (2) Hostility to Judaism | 152 |
|    (3) Attempt to Allegorise the Gospel History | 152 |
|    (4) Transformation of the Theory of Redemption | 154 |
|    (5) Aversion to the Jewish Millenium | 155 |
|    (6) Limited number who could be Saved | 155 |
|    (7) The Threefold Discipline | 156 |
| § 4. Marcion | 157 |
|    (1) His Religious Aim | 157 |
|    (2) His New Testament | 158 |
|    (3) The Weak Point in his System | 159 |

## CHAPTER VII.

### THE RISE OF THE CATHOLIC CHURCH.

| | |
|---|---|
| § 1 Organisation of the Early Churches | 160 |
|    (1) No Officials charged with the Duty of Teaching | 160 |
|    (2) Bishops and Deacons: Presbyters or 'Elders' | 161 |
|    (3) Concentration of Authority in the Bishops | 162 |
|       (a) The Bishop or Presbyter becomes a Teacher | 162 |
|       (b) One Bishop to one Church | 162 |
|    (4) The Bishops as Successors of the Apostles | 163 |

## TABLE OF CONTENTS

|  | PAGE. |
|---|---|
| § 2. The World-wide Federation of the Bishops | 164 |
| (1) Growth of a Politico-Religious Union reflecting the Civil Constitution of the Empire | 164 |
| (2) The Foundations of the Primacy of Rome | 165 |
| § 3. The Work of the New Church | 168 |
| (1) The Bishops enforce the 'Rule of Faith' | 168 |
| (2) The Canon of the New Testament | 170 |
| (3) The Apostolic Tradition replaced the Sense of Present Inspiration | 172 |
| § 4. Growth of Speculative Theology | 173 |
| (1) The Earliest 'Rule of Faith' says nothing of the Deity of Christ | 173 |
| (2) New Doctrinal Questions started | 173 |
| (3) Protests in favour of the Sole Godhead of the Father | 174 |
| (4) Identity of Christ with the Father | 175 |
| (5) Paul of Samosata | 176 |
| (6) Change in the Basis of Christian Union | 177 |
| § 5. Christian Mysteries | 178 |
| (1) Analogies between Catholic Worship and the Mysteries | 178 |
| (a) Baptism | 179 |
| (b) The Eucharist | 180 |
| (2) The Christian Priesthood | 180 |
| § 6. The Relaxation of Discipline | 182 |
| (1) Decline of Rigour: Novatian's Protest | 182 |
| (2) Monachism as a Reaction against the Domination of the Priesthood | 183 |

## CHAPTER VIII.

### IMPENDING TRIUMPH OF THE MIXED SYSTEM.

| Vitality and Growth of the Church | 185 |
|---|---|
| § 1. Foreign Elements brought into Christianity | 187 |
| (1) Adaptation of Ideas of Morality and Philosophy | 187 |

## TABLE OF CONTENTS

§ 1. Foreign Elements brought into Christianity (*continued*)—
 (2) Greek Rhetoric and the Christian Sermon . 187
 (3) Civilisation of the Empire handed on through the Church. . . . . . . 188
 (4) Compromise with the Polytheism of the Empire . . . . . . . 189

§ 2. Intrinsic Strength of Christianity . . . . 190
 (1) Mere Adaptation insufficient to explain the Church's Triumph . . . . . 190
 (2) Superiority of Historic Fact to Speculation . 191
 (3) The Manifestation of a Divine Life . . 192
 (4) Counter Attempt to produce a Philosophic Ideal: Apollonius of Tyana . . . 193

§ 3. The Power of Christianity over the Heart . . . 194
 (1) Compared with the Stoic Morality . . 194
 (2) As a Religion for all Classes and Grades of Education . . . . . . . 195
 (3) As the Religion of the Poor . . . . 196

§ 4. Limitations to the Efficacy of Christianity . . . 198
 (1) Defects of Christian Morality . . . 198
 (2) Nevertheless Superior to the Average Morality 199
 (3) Bad Effects of Dogma chiefly confined to its Constructors . . . . . . 200
 (4) The Canon of the New Testament preserved Christianity from complete Corruption . 200

APPENDIX A, Table of Roman Emperors . . . . 203
APPENDIX B, Chief Points in the Church History of the First Three Centuries . . . . . 206
 First Period . . . . . . . . 206
 Second Period . . . . . . . 208
 Third Period . . . . . . . . 210
APPENDIX C . . . . . . . . . . 213
 (1) Heathen Writers . . . . . . 213
 (2) Christian Literature . . . . . 214

# CHRISTIANITY

AND THE

ROMAN EMPIRE

# CHAPTER I.

## THE ROMAN EMPIRE.

EARLY Christian writers thought, and very naturally, that the Roman Empire arose in the providence of God in order that the gospel might be preached to all nations. The Apostles, says Origen, would have had much more difficulty in fulfilling this command, if the nations had been subject to many masters and so had lived in mutual enmity and suspicion.[1] The fact that the unity of many nations under the Roman government promoted the spread of Christianity is evident enough: indeed it is hard to see how Christianity could have won its signal victory over heathenism, had the political situation been other than it was. There are, however, two other facts which seriously modify the view of the modern historian, and which Origen neither did nor could take into his reckoning. In the first place, the Roman Empire did not, of course, embrace the whole world, but only

[1] Origen, *Against Celsus*, ii. 30. Comp. Eusebius, *Demonstr. Evang.* iii. 6.

B

covered a small part of its extent. To this limited area the Christian religion was almost exclusively confined during the first three centuries of its existence. Even now it is not the religion of the world: it is true that it was adopted by the Teutonic races and by some of the Celts and Slavs, who had never fallen under the discipline of Roman rule, but, with these exceptions, Christianity at this day is the religion professed by those who descend from the subjects of Imperial Rome. In the second place the Roman Empire was by no means the passive recipient of Christianity. If on the one hand it accepted Christian ideas, on the other, Christianity, long before it became the religion of the Empire, had incorporated the most important elements of the Graeco-Roman civilisation and was profoundly affected for good and for evil by the change. It was this transformed Christianity which took possession of the Empire, and which was imparted by Roman or Romanised missionaries to the Teutonic and Sclavonic nations. Thus, the Roman Empire never died: it lived on, it lives still in the theology and institutions of the Catholic church which was its heir. The Reformation of the sixteenth century was an attempt to discard these later accretions and to restore primitive Christianity. It was only among the Northern races, which had never been subject to Rome, that this movement had any considerable success. Moreover, the reform was exceedingly imperfect, and the most radical of the Protestant churches retained much which was not Christian but Roman. Hence the importance of our subject: apart from the Roman Empire, its political and social life, we necessarily fail to understand the history of Christianity. We must begin then by trying to see what that political and social life was.

### § 1. The Geographical limits of the Empire.

The territory of the Empire, as Augustus left it, extended from the Euphrates on the east to the Atlantic on the west, from the deserts of Arabia and Africa on the south to the Rhine and Danube on the north. In the midst lay the great central basin of the Mediterranean Sea, and the Roman arms had subdued Asia Minor, Syria, Egypt, a narrow strip of coast along the southern side of the Mediterranean from Egypt to the straits of Gibraltar, and, north of the Mediterranean, the countries now known as Turkey in Europe and Greece with Bulgaria, Servia, and Bosnia, Italy and the islands in the Mediterranean, Spain and Portugal, France and Belgium, Germany west of the Rhine, Switzerland, and Austria south of the Danube. The space given measured something like 2,000 miles from north to south, and 3,000 from east to west. It is supposed to have contained about 100 million inhabitants.[1]

Compared with the extent and population of the globe, these figures may well seem insignificant. The Russian dominion stretches further now than the Roman Empire did of old, and British India surpasses the Roman Empire in population. But such standards of comparison are quite inadequate. All the elements of human progress were found within the limits of the Empire;

[1] So Hertzberg in Riehm's *Bibel Wörterbuch*, Art. Rom.

and the civilisations of the far east, those for example
of India and China, are of little account when set side
by side with that of Rome. To the subject of the
Roman Empire these distant lands were scarcely known.
He had indeed good cause to remember the existence
of the Parthian Kingdom beyond the Euphrates, for
the Parthians were formidable enemies of Rome, and
so were the Persians who rose to power on the ruins
of the Parthian state in 226 A.D. But the Parthians
and Persians were semi-barbarous, and as for the rest
of the world with which the Roman had any real
acquaintance, it was either sunk in savagery or raised
but one step above it. As yet, no one dreamt of the
future which was in store for the Teutonic tribes in
Northern Europe. The Roman was content to stem
the current of barbarian invasion. The successors
of Augustus acquiesced in the advice which he had
bequeathed them and seldom made any serious attempt
to widen the boundaries of the Empire. To this general
rule there were however two notable exceptions. During
the first century after Christ, Britain so far north as
the Tyne and the Solway became a Roman province.
At the beginning of the second century Trajan added
the great province of Dacia, a vast district some 1,300
miles in circumference to the north of the lower Danube.
But the important point to remember is that the
imagination of a Roman subject travelled little beyond
the limits of the Empire. To him the Empire and
the world were practically identical. 'The world
itself,' so Tertullian writes, 'lies before us. All is now
'open, all is known, all is occupied with trade.'[1]

[1] Tertullian, *On the Soul*, 30.

## § 2. The Unity of the Empire.

(1) This unity could not be permanently secured except by the absolute rule of one man. Not that political freedom and democracy were unknown to Greeks and Romans: on the contrary they had attained a very high degree of development among them. But the conception of representative government had not as yet arisen. Democracy was taken in the proper and literal sense: it meant the direct and immediate rule of the people. Questions of peace and war or of internal administration were decided by the public assembly of the people and not by a chamber of their representatives. Such a method of government was possible, so long as the state did not extend beyond a city and its adjacent district, though even then it could not perhaps have been realised, had it not been for the presence of slaves, who had of course no share in public life, and left the free citizens a certain amount of leisure. But when the Roman Empire began to be, democracy was doomed. 'Where the Roman 'conquered, he settled.'[1] In other words, colonies of Roman citizens were distributed all over the known world. Add to this that all free inhabitants of Italy had been admitted to the Roman franchise, so that a popular assembly could not include more than an insignificant fraction of those who were legally entitled to vote. It was not conceivable, that Romans all over the world would leave the management of their affairs to the mob in the Roman city. Rule might be exercised

[1] Seneca, *Consol. ad Helv.* 7.

by an oligarchy, by the members of wealthy families, or by men whose talents had brought them to the front. And for a long time this method was tried but with disastrous results. The provinces were ruthlessly plundered by Senators who turned their brief lease of power to the best advantage, and made room for successors as unscrupulous as themselves. There was besides the danger of civil war between rival leaders eager for domination, a danger which again and again became a terrible reality. The end of all this was inevitable, though it was long in coming. One supreme head was necessary for the army, and the head of the army must be the head of the State. This change was finally accomplished in 31 B.C., when Augustus became sole and absolute ruler of the Roman world. The new form of government was welcome to the world at large, however much aristocratic dreamers might regret the disappearance of the Republic. The Republic had fallen by its own weight: twenty years of civil war had devastated the Empire, and the new order brought peace and prosperity everywhere, but especially in the provinces. No serious attempt was ever made to revive the Republican constitution.

(2) In form that constitution was still maintained—and Augustus was much too wise to assume the hated title of King. His private life was that of an ordinary citizen, and his sovereignty was attained by the accumulation of old and legitimate offices in his single person and by their renewal during his lifetime. But in reality the Emperor was absolute. Even the pretence of convoking the assembly of the Roman people ceased with the death of Augustus. The

legislative power was transferred to the Senate, an assembly which under Augustus consisted of five or six hundred persons, representing the aristocracy of wealth. Its powers were very great; not only did it make laws, it also formed the final court of appeal in civil causes and in criminal causes likewise, if they were concerned with crimes dangerous to the public weal. When an Emperor died, the Senate was supposed to choose his successor. Those provinces which did not need military protection from the barbarians, or were not, like Egypt and Judæa, specially impatient of Roman law, were committed to the care of the Senate and governed by Proconsuls who were chosen annually by lot from the members of that body. In reality, however, the power of the Senate depended on the good-will of the prince. He had power to revise the Senatorial list, and constitutional freedom is impossible when the executive authority nominates the legislative body. The Emperor was assisted by a sort of Privy Council consisting of some twenty members. Gradually the theory of Republican Government was surrendered. Early in the third century A.D. the Praetorian troops (originally the Emperor's body-guard) had grown into a force of 50,000 men, superior in arms and appointments to any force that could be brought against them. The Praetorian Prefect from a simple captain in the guards became the chief administrator of law and finance. Soldiers ceased to be recruited in Italy, and its inhabitants lost all fitness for war. Servile Orientals were promoted to the Senate: Orientals ascended the Imperial throne. The Emperor's power depended upon his success in pleasing the army and it was hardly worth while to maintain the empty form of consulting the Senate. In these circumstances we cannot wonder that an elaborate theory of despotism was constructed by the great jurists of the Empire, by Papinian, Paulus, Ulpian. In reality, the old Roman Empire may be said to have expired with M. Aurelius in 180.

(3) Except among Jews and Egyptians there was no real wish for the recovery of national life and independence. The Roman Imperialism was felt to be a blessing, because it ensured the priceless boon of public peace. In one respect the subjects of Rome were better off than the present inhabitants of European countries. We see around us nations armed to the teeth, and enduring heavy taxation to support immense armaments. Under the Roman Empire no such necessity existed. The whole civilised world was one, and although there were masses of barbarians in the unknown lands beyond the Rhine, the Danube, and the Euphrates, these gave comparatively little trouble during the first two and a half centuries. It is true that things changed for the worse under Decius, who in the year 251 fell in battle against the Goths, and his successors had to carry on the same desperate struggle which first exhausted and finally destroyed the fabric of the Empire. Nevertheless, for nearly the whole of the period with which we have to deal, public peace was secured, and this by an army and navy which together did not number more than 450,000 men. On the other hand, the Empire was again and again torn by civil war which was almost inevitable, since the principle of hereditary rule was not recognised. Still this want was to a considerable extent remedied

by the principle of adoption. In this manner the Emperor with more or less deference to public opinion really nominated his successor. During the two centuries which elapsed between the accession of Augustus and the death of Commodus, there was little blood shed in civil war, the chief exception being the eighteen months which followed Nero's death. After Domitian's death in 96, the Imperial power was held for nearly a century by a line of wise and benevolent rulers. It must be remembered too that bad men like Tiberius did little, if any, harm to the provinces: it was eminent persons in immediate contact with them who suffered from their tyranny. It was, of course, otherwise, during the latter part of our period, when the dangers from barbarians, and, as a consequence of this, the increased power of the army and the weight of taxation, caused severe social strain.

(4) Further, the unity of the Empire was consolidated by a magnificent system of law, the like of which the world had never seen before, and which is still a main factor in our modern civilisation. It was a great thing to be a Roman citizen. It implied the right of making a will, of inheritance, of marriage protected by public sanction: it carried with it the privilege of appeal to the law courts, and raised the happy possessor of the franchise to a state in which his life and property were guarded from outrage and wrong. ' Often and 'in many lands had the mere words, "I am a Roman 'citizen," brought help and security among foreigners.'[1] It opened the road to the highest honours in the State. The rights of Roman citizenship were extended by

[1] Cicero, *In Verr.* v. 57.

degrees, though it was not till the reign of Caracalla in the year 215 A.D. that all free inhabitants of the provinces became Roman citizens. But during the two preceding centuries, the rights of citizenship were within the reach of a very moderate ambition. They might be given as the reward of merit: they might be purchased: they belonged as of right to the magistrates of many provincial cities. It is probable that during the middle of the second century the larger part of the free population possessed the full rights of citizenship. This counts for little, if we regard the franchise from the modern point of view, and consider it as a share in the election of the governing body. The Roman citizen exercised no such right. But he had the inestimable advantage of trial by just laws: he had attained a state of dignity and independence of which Orientals had never dreamt, while they lived under their own kings. Again, though the provincial cities had no voice in the administration of the Empire, they had a large measure of freedom in the administration of their own affairs. It was not till the reign of Diocletian, towards the close of the third century, that the provinces were oppressed by extreme centralisation of government. We can well understand the tone of grateful respect which the New Testament and Christian writers of a later day maintain to the Roman rule. The Roman jurisprudence answered its purpose, because it had been constructed by the genius of great lawyers to meet the necessities of a great Empire, composed of many nationalities. It was based on the general principles found in all existing systems of law: local and arbitrary elements were gradually eliminated, and the complicated system which had satisfied the wants of the early Romans, because it was endeared to them by use and wont, but which would have been an intolerable burden to foreigners, was replaced by a *jus gentium*, the common law of nations. Stoic philosophers with their conceptions of human equality and a universal state had their part in this great work, and helped to make the law what it claimed to be, the embodiment of natural reason. It was enforced with discretion and with wise allowance for national customs and prejudice. Slowly, but surely, it made its way, and recommended itself by its intrinsic superiority.

(5) The Empire was one in virtue of its central authority which controlled it, and the system of law which prevailed throughout its territory. There were other bonds which held it together. Modern nationalities are parted by language, but in the Roman world two languages prevailed nearly everywhere. The Western provinces were Latinised. So completely for example had Spain and Gaul adopted the Latin tongue that the languages originally spoken in these countries have perished : modern French, for instance, is a daughter of Latin, and retains few and doubtful fragments of the old Celtic speech. Spain produced famous ' Latin authors, viz: Columella, Seneca, Lucan, Martial, Quintilian, and one of the best of Roman Emperors, viz: Trajan. Greek was the language familiar to the whole East, with the partial exceptions of Syria and Egypt, and it was understood by educated persons all the world over. The Greek literature, and the Latin which had been formed after its model, had no rivals;

the Jews alone could be said to possess a literature apart. Further, great lines of road connected the most distant extremities, and public officers could travel by post at the rate of a hundred miles in the day. By land and sea there was constant interchange of commodities, and in its better days the Empire was saved from the famines which had often afflicted the infant Republic. This led naturally to a fusion of all races in the great centres of trade, in cities such as Ephesus, Corinth, Antioch, and above all in Rome. Hence, in the cities, where Christianity spread at first, national life was undermined and could offer comparatively little opposition to the new and universal religion.

### § 3. The Influence of Religion.

It must not, however, be thought that Christianity merely filled a vacuum and met with little resistance. In a subsequent chapter we shall consider the legal opposition which crossed its path. Meantime, it is necessary to speak of two great forces, which exercised wide and powerful influence. In part they promoted the progress of Christianity, in part they retarded it very seriously. These forces were heathen religion and philosophy. They intermingled with each other but we shall consider them, so far as that is possible, apart.

(1) First, then, with regard to heathen religion. It was exceedingly vigorous during the whole of our period and beyond it.

(a) No doubt, the Roman literature at the close of the Republic and during the Augustan age affords some justification for the theory that religious belief was dying out among the educated classes. The Epicurean Lucretius attacked religion fiercely, and Horace, an Epicurean of less serious disposition, was certainly very far from any deep sense of religion. But literary men cannot safely be taken as representatives of the general sentiment, and besides there were other literary men of the same time, Cicero, for example, and Virgil, whose attitude to the traditional religion was much more respectful. Even those who had perhaps little faith of their own, acknowledged the need of religion for the masses, or were disposed to maintain it on grounds of public policy. Women and the common people, says Strabo, cannot be led to piety by philosophic reasoning, 'they need superstition.'[1] Maecenas is said to have advised Augustus to promote religion, because those who despised that, would make light of all authority.

(b) But during the first three centuries of the Empire there was a positive revival of the ancient religions. Able and enlightened princes such as Hadrian and the Antonines were conspicuous for their religious zeal. M. Aurelius, the philosophic Emperor, was sedulous in his sacrifices. When he was with the army on the Danube, he flung live lions into the river at the instigation of a famous soothsayer, Alexander of Abonoteichos. A wit of the day made the white cattle which were chosen for sacrifices after victory, address the pious Emperor in the words, 'If thou dost win, we are lost.' The

[1] Strabo, 1, 2, p. 19 c.

satirical writer Lucian, who wrote in the second century, mocked at religious observances, but he stood nearly alone, and he confesses, that 'most of the Greeks, the rabble and all the barbarians,'[1] were on the other side.

(c) Nor was it the noble only who clung to the old views. In all likelihood the number of educated persons who discarded superstition utterly was very small. Here and there one might have met an Epicurean like Lucian, or a man of dry and rationalistic spirit like the elder Pliny, the natural historian. But there was no reason why an educated man of those times should distrust stories of the marvellous. The conception of natural law with its universal dominion was foreign to the ancient world. The Stoic, the Platonist, the Pythagorean philosophies, accepted the popular myths, only purging them of their grosser and immoral elements. Certainly, tales of prodigies and omens found ready listeners among all classes. Tacitus is the last writer whom one would accuse of weakness or aptitude for superstition: yet he tells with perfect gravity, and with a faith which is evidently sincere, the story of an ominous bird which foreboded the death of the Emperor Otho. Indeed, he says frankly, that he thinks it beneath the dignity of history to search for idle tales, but on the other hand he does not dare to disbelieve marvels, when well attested.[2]

(d) The confident belief of Celsus is still more striking. This well-known opponent of Christianity was a contemporary of M. Aurelius. He was a man

---

[1] Lucian, *Jup. Tragœd.* ad fin.
[2] Tacitus, *Hist.* ii. 50.

of wide culture, of philosophical tastes, experienced in the world, and, though partly inclined to Platonism, a friend of the sceptical Lucian. Nevertheless, he confidently appeals in his attack on Christianity to the innumerable oracles and omens verified by the event, to miraculous cures, divine apparitions, supernatural vengeance meted out to the profane. 'All life,' he cries, 'is full of these 'things.'[1] Very slight evidence or rather no evidence at all, if we judge by modern standards, sufficed as proof of the supernatural. A sudden storm relieved a Roman legion under the command of M. Aurelius, when distressed with thirst. A heathen historian, Dio Cassius, who wrote in the same generation, attributed the storm to the power of an Egyptian sorcerer; others thought it was given in answer to the prayers of the pious Emperor; while Christians boldly assumed that deliverance was obtained by the supplication of Christian soldiers, and made the story more marvellous by the addition of extraordinary incidents which flagrantly contradict the sober facts of history. For the present, however, our concern is with heathenism. The belief in the Heathen gods must have been strong, when men were so ready to recognise their supernatural power.

(2) The religion of the day was no longer the old religion of the Roman city. That religion still survived. Importance was still attached to the auguries, and to the sacrifices which the magistrates offered in the name of the State. The Arval brothers still chanted their song in Latin of immemorial antiquity and made their procession through the fields; the same colleges of

[1] Origen, *Against Celsus*, viii. 45.

priests performed the same sacred rites for more than a thousand years, till the edict of Theodosius at the end of the fourth century forbade their continuance. Nay, the old religion put forth fresh shoots under the Empire. A new goddess, Annona, presided over the supply of corn which came from the provinces to Rome. The worship of the Emperor's genius or guardian spirit was a genuine development of the old Roman worship. That worship gave little play to mythological fancy. It set up a series of dry abstractions, but it made much of reverence, of order in the family and state: each detail of private and public life had its protecting deity. The 'genius of the Roman people' had been adored as early at least as the second Punic war (219–202 B.C.). It was, therefore, by a very natural logic that this cult was transferred to the genius of the Emperor, when the powers of the State were united in him. This worship became the central point of the State religion, and, Roman though it was in origin, was promoted by the servile spirit of the east. As a rule, it was after their death that Emperors and their relatives formally obtained divine honours; as many as thirty-seven canonisations of this kind took place during the first four centuries of the Empire.

(3) There was, however, a vast amount of popular worship practised in all Roman lands, and in Rome itself, which was utterly alien to the spirit of the old Roman religion. Polytheism is tolerant: a man's devotion to the gods of his country did not hinder him from recognising the gods of other countries. When the barriers of national life were broken down, gods of many nationalities were mingled together. The

Roman religion was above all things a State religion: it offered little satisfaction to individual needs. Now, the mixed population of the Empire was too cosmopolitan to be patriotic. Soldiers and merchants who passed from land to land, adopted and spread the worship of foreign deities. It was eastern rites which attracted the most numerous and zealous devotees. It was in vain that Tiberius tried to stem the enthusiasm for the Egyptian goddess Isis at Rome. Inscriptions still bear witness to her universal popularity, in Spain and Gaul, in Germany, in Greece, in Asia Minor. About the year 200 A.D., the Persian sun-god Mithra, long known to the Romans, became the most popular deity of all, and held his ground for two centuries.

(4) For several reasons these later cults have an intense interest for the student of early Christianity. They were often associated with gross sensuality and imposture, with the credulity which was, as we have seen, characteristic of the times. But we must not forget that they satisfied real wants, to some extent rational wants of human nature. They were something more than additions to the crowd of deities, numerous enough already. Isis and Serapis were each identified in pantheistic fashion with the one divine principle of which all popular deities were the symbols ot the manifestation. Hence the attraction which the worship of Isis exercised over an able statesman like Hadrian or a philosopher like Plutarch. The worship of Mithra was the nearest approach to Monotheism which the Roman Empire made before it adopted Christianity. The old sun-god had become the lord of life and death, the protector and the guide. The Roman State, as

has been said, was bound up with an antique worship. But now the claims of individual life were asserting themselves. A desire awoke for forgiveness of sins, for a life beyond the grave. Men craved for a religion which could create enthusiasm and satisfy love. The Roman Empire conferred many benefits, but how could a Greek or Syrian love a government in which he had neither part nor lot? The new worship promised to fulfil these desires. It had its sacrament of pardon. The worshipper was placed in a pit: an ox or ram was slain over his head: he was bathed in the blood which dropped upon him through perforated beams, and went away purified from sin. It satisfied the craving for sympathy. The worshippers met in small chapels, often underground; they formed a secret society in which each was bound to each by common faith and hope and discipline: they were subjected to asceticism so severe that some died under it. The initiated were divided into different grades and there was a hierarchy with a 'father of fathers' at the head of it. Painted representations of their common meal were discovered in a crypt near the Porta S. Sebastiano at Rome, and were at first mistaken for Christian love-feasts. The initiated were assured of a happy immortality. 'Be 'of good courage,' said the priest, as he anointed them with holy oil: 'Be of good courage, ye that have been 'saved by God: after your toils salvation will be yours.'

(5) The social and voluntary character of this worship strikes us at once: in this respect it offers the most obvious contrast to the old Roman religion in which the consul sacrificed for the State, or the father for the family. Here, however, the worshippers of Mithra

were not original ; they were merely touched by the spirit of association which was then in the air. In every part of the Empire people formed clubs or societies. They had their trades unions, their dramatic clubs, their friendly societies, their literary associations. The impulse to association was so strong, that the State felt obliged to regulate and sometimes to repress it. Now it is to be observed that these clubs were in some cases directly religious, in nearly all cases were placed under the sanction of religion. They replaced the cold formalism of the official religion by the fervour which belonged then as now to small assemblies, where every man is bound to his brother, and in that proportion separated from the outer world. Women and slaves were admitted to the worship of the chapel, and met as equals at the fraternal meal. To some extent, at least, the members of these clubs seem to have been bound together by moral aspirations. An extant code of rules which has survived requires the officers to see whether the candidate for admission be 'chaste and 'pious and good.' It is a pathetic feature in these associations that many of them were intended to secure decent burial for their members. The ashes of the brethren were set side by side, and there were pious unions in which the bond of brotherhood was believed to continue after death.

#### 4. Philosophy.

While the poorer classes found their comfort in religious association, many of the richer and better educated sought it in philosophy.

(1) The functions of a philosopher, under the Empire, were strangely unlike all that the name suggests, or chiefly suggests, to us. The philosopher spoke to the public, who gathered in schools which were sometimes, though not always, open without fee. There he did the office of a modern preacher. According to Epictetus a school of philosophy was the consulting room of a physician. Men came to the philosopher with maladies of the soul. It was an abuse to look for fine speeches and sounding phrases, for the real object was to depart cured, or on the way to cure. Philosophers also acted as wandering preachers who went from place to place, and called men from the storm of passion to purity and inward peace. They were the advisers of statesmen; the best of the Emperors, Nerva, Trajan, Hadrian, the Antonines, were surrounded by philosophers. They were the confessors and directors of the great. Canius Julus went to execution accompanied by his philospher: Rubellius Plautus and Thrasea in their last moments were sustained by the philosophers who were their spiritual guides.[1] The philosopher, moreover, figured as a kind of family chaplain, and waited upon some lady of wealth who affected philosophy, because it was in vogue. Such a position, of course,

---

[1] Tacitus, *Ann.* xiv. 59; Seneca, *Tranquill. Anim.* 14; Tacitus, *Ann.* xvi. 34.

must often have exposed him to a degradation which he had brought upon himself.

(2) How was it that philosophy came to play such strange parts? The answer is that philosophy had changed its character and aims. It was no longer a speculative system which strove to account for things by examining ultimate causes. Such was the philosophy of Plato and Aristotle. Such was not the philosophy of Zeno or Epicurus. Greek speculation died out after the death of Greek freedom. Zeno and Epicurus asked how is a man to order his life? What must he do or not do that he may live well? The one put the end of life in virtue, the other in pleasure. But the spirit of each was practical, not speculative. Even the counsel given by the one, resembled that given by the other. Seek freedom from passion, said Zeno. Seek freedom from mental disturbance, said Epicurus.

(3) We may dismiss Epicureanism, which had no permanent influence in the Empire, and look more closely at Stoicism.

Zeno, who has been just mentioned, was the founder of the school. He taught at Athens about 300 B.C. in the *Stoa Poikilé*, or frescoed arcade, from which his disciples took their name. His teaching was developed by Chrysippus, who was esteemed the second founder of the school, and who died an old man in 206 B.C. It is remarkable that no eminent Stoic was Greek by blood. Zeno and Chrysippus were both Orientals, and lacked that capacity for speculative thought which was proper to the Greeks. Their philosophy was a materialistic Pantheism, borrowed chiefly from Heraclitus; their ethics were taken from the Cynics. All knowledge, they held, came from sense: only matter had real existence. God was the soul of the world, in substance an ethereal fire permeating all, directing all for the common good, but doing so in accordance with inexorable fate which took no thought of the individual as such. God was all in all, for from this ethereal fire which they called God, all things had proceeded: it was continually reducing everything to itself. At last came the general conflagration and the cycles of being began over again, for matter was eternal and could change its form only, not its substance. The reason in man, his guiding principle, was part of the world-soul, *i.e.* of God. Man had one duty, to live according to nature. But what is nature? It is the reason of the world, the reason which is in each man, the common reason expressed in the moral sentiments of mankind. This virtue or compliance with nature is the only good, while vice is the only evil. Thus the wise man quells his passions and despises alike the pleasure and pain, which are the motives of the uneducated.

(*b*) This philosophy was transplanted to Rome long before the Christian era. But it flourished chiefly under the Empire, when Seneca, Musonius, Epictetus, M. Aurelius, gave it its greatest names. On Roman soil Stoicism underwent remarkable modifications. The value of the earlier Stoicism lay in its moral earnestness. Yet it had its physics, and above all it cultivated logic with minute and wearisome pedantry. The Roman Stoics frankly declared the small interest they took in any questions, save questions of duty. 'What does 'it profit,' asks Seneca, 'to know which line is straight, 'if you don't know what is the straight course in life?'[1]

[1] Seneca, *Ep.* lxxxviii.

'These enquiries make us learned, not good: wisdom 'is a more obvious, aye a simpler thing.'[1] Again, Seneca, for all his declamation on the self-sufficiency of the sage, painfully felt that this ideal condition of mind was never realised. His Stoicism too contained elements borrowed from different philosophies. Under the Empire philosophies mingled, as religions mingled—and Seneca, in this more like a Platonist than a Stoic, looks on the body as the prison of the soul, and in his view of human sinfulness and 'the flesh'[2] his utterances often tally in the most astonishing way with those of St. Paul. The later Stoics did not abandon the materialist Pantheism of their founders—and when Seneca acknowledges the need of divine help, his language is probably much more Christian than his thought. To him the reason of man was part of the universal reason which sustained the universe. Thus, if on the one hand, the sage humbled himself before God, on the other he felt that he was the equal of deity: nay, in one way he was according to Seneca its superior, because he attained virtue by his own effort.[3] Again, though the later Stoics use language which sounds like Monotheism, they did not dream of discarding the popular mythology, except where it was immoral. Their system left room for many deities, each of which embodied a portion of the divine spirit. The Stoic did not look upon death as the end of all. The soul still survived and continued its personal life; only, however, till the impending conflagration of the world, when its individuality would be absorbed into that of the universal spirit. For the rest, deliverance from

[1] *Ep.* cvi.   [2] *Ep.* lxv.   [3] *Ep.* liii.

the body was a gain, not a loss, in the eyes of the later Stoics. 'It is but the image of your son which 'has perished,' so Seneca writes to a bereaved parent, 'he himself is eternal,' (here he goes beyond rigid Stoicism) 'and is in a better condition.'[1]

But the true beauty of Stoicism, and especially of the later Stoicism, was its humanity. The upright mind, says Seneca, is nothing else than God dwelling in a mortal body, and such a mind may be found alike in a Roman Knight, in a freedman, in a slave.[2] 'Slave,' says Epictetus to the cruel slave-owner, 'wilt 'thou not bear with thine own brother? Wilt thou not 'remember who thou art and over whom thou hast 'power, that they are thy kinsfolk, thy brethren by 'nature, the descendants of Zeus?'[3] When scourged the perfect sage will love his tormentors, knowing that he is the 'father and brother of all.'[4] These fine sayings on the brotherhood of man are something better than declamatory phrases, though allowance must be made for the rhetorical spirit of the age. The gentle disposition of M. Aurelius was deeply affected by the feeling of human brotherhood. Here are a few of his maxims. 'I cannot find it in my heart to be angry with one 'of my own nature or family,' (*i.e.* with any man) 'for we 'are all made for mutual help, as the feet, the hands, 'the eyelids.' 'A man that has done a kindness never 'proclaims it, but does another as soon as he can, 'like the vine which bears again the next season.' 'The 'best way of revenge is not to imitate the injury.' 'Mankind are under one common law, and, if so, they

---

[1] *Consol. ad Marc.* xxiv.   [2] *Ep.* xxxi. ad fin.
[3] Epictetus, *Diss.* i. 13.   [4] *Diss.* iii. 22, 54.

'must be fellow-citizens.'[1] Stoic principles, too, had a great influence on public weal. The Roman lawyers eagerly adopted the Stoic idea of a universal State, and gave it expression in the Roman code. Despite its theories of equality, however, Stoicism did not rise to the thought of a world without slaves : it was not till centuries were gone that Christian imagination took so bold a flight. But under Hadrian and the Antonines slaves were for the first time placed under the protection of the law. Their owners lost the power of life and death; they could no longer kill their slaves unchallenged; the subterraneous dungeons were abolished, and in case of intolerable hardship a slave could obtain his freedom, or at least secure transference to a better master. It is, moreover, to the credit of Stoicism that Seneca is the one Roman writer who expressed disapproval of those gladiatorial shows which Roman ladies witnessed without shame.

(4) Stoicism in this modified form was for long the chief, though not the only philosophy. The four great philosophies, viz: the Platonic, the Aristotelian, the Stoic, and the Epicurean, were all represented in the chairs which the Antonines founded and endowed at Athens. Of these the Aristotelians and Epicureans need not detain our attention, but of the Platonists something must be said. Their best representative was the famous and voluminous writer Plutarch of Chaeronea, in Boeotia, who died 120 A.D. A Platonist in the true sense he was not. A Platonist was impossible during an age so poor in speculative thought. His

[1] See the introduction to the English translation of M. Aurelius by Alice Zimmern.

interest was occupied by morality and religion, and though he borrowed from any philosophy suited to his purpose, his best inspirations were caught from the Platonic philosophy. He developed the Platonic idea of the divine unity: he inherited the Platonic dualism which tended to place the origin of evil in matter, and he found the way to religious contentment in rising to union with God by a moral and ascetic life. His Monotheism, however, allowed him to recognise a vast multitude of gods and demons who were the secondary objects of religious worship. He himself officiated as a heathen priest.

(5) More than a hundred years after Plutarch's death Platonism entered on another phase and attained a most remarkable degree of popularity. In this new form it is known as Neoplatonism. Ammonius Saccas who died in 245 is generally regarded as the founder of the School. His most famous scholar Plotinus was born in Egypt in the year 205, came to Rome in 244 and found numerous disciples there, among whom were the Emperor Gallienus and his wife. He died in 270; his writings were arranged by his distinguished pupil Porphyry, and in that form still survive. Neoplatonism has really little claim to the name of a philosophy. Yet it arose from the same want which philosophy professes to satisfy; it endeavoured to supply a basis of certainty. The old beliefs had been shaken by scepticism. Amidst the variety of opinion and usage prevalent in the Empire, how could one be sure of anything? The Stoics had answered much as the Scotch philosophy answered the scepticism of Berkeley and Hume. They appealed to the 'common conceptions' of mankind. This was

casting out scepticism by scepticism, for acquiescence in untested opinion is the negation of philosophy. No Plato or Aristotle arose to solve the problem. But the Neoplatonists, despairing of philosophy, took refuge in religion, or rather in revelation. They believed that traces of divine inspiration were to be found among all nations. But the more ancient a worship was, or professed to be, the richer, as the Neoplatonists thought, was its treasure of divine wisdom. They were specially attracted by the ancient worships of the east. But to them every form of polytheism, when an allegorical method of interpretation had refined the grossness of its mythology, was holy and venerable. Their philosophy tended more and more to become not philosophy, but a theosophy. Revelation was the basis of certainty. The philosopher had also to pursue personal holiness. The ethics of the Neoplatonists were borrowed from the Stoics. Besides this the strictest asceticism was enjoined: abstinence from flesh and wine, and a single life, were means of perfection. The philosopher was to withdraw himself from the multiplicity of things to the unity of reason. This, however, was not enough. God is above reason, beyond all thought. The highest bliss was reached, when thought ceased, and the philosopher in ecstatic vision was united to the cause of all being and all good. Plotinus, during the six years that Porphyry spent with him, was rapt into ecstasy four times.

## § 5. Summary of Results.

To sum up. The age which preceded and accompanied the growth of Christianity was an age in which men, ideas, things, were mingled together. The partition walls between nation and nation were pulled down, and the belief in the unity of mankind was strong. The spirit of genuine speculation was dead: the literary splendour of Greece and Rome was fading away, and sense and taste alike were spoiled by garish rhetoric. But on the other hand, we find philosophers of many schools contributing to form an ideal of virtuous life. We find an increased spirit of humanity, which shows itself in the improved condition of slaves, in institutions for destitute children, in benevolent confraternities. We find an intermingling of all religions, and, partly as a result of this, a general tendency to Monotheism: so that men retain the belief in many gods, but regard them more and more as manifestations of one divine spirit. Finally, we see in Neoplatonism an attempt to merge philosophy in religion, and particular religions in one universal religion.

# CHAPTER II.

## THE CHRISTIAN MISSION.

### § 1. Why the Christian Mission travelled Westwards.

IN the year 51 A.D., St. Paul had already preached Christ among the Gentiles, and his efforts had met with a success which compelled the older disciples to recognise the spread of the gospel among the heathen as an accomplished fact. From that time onwards the work of conversion advanced, and always or almost always in one direction. The good news travelled from east to west: it travelled along the shores of the Mediterranean sea, and Christianity established its first outposts in the towns which were within a moderate distance of the coast. The reasons for this are not far to seek.

(1) The Romans had swept away the pirates which had once infested the great inland sea, and had opened an easy and secure passage to the traveller. Again, Christian missionaries journeyed west, because the Roman Empire lay west of Palestine, which had been the birth-place of the new religion. Within the Empire

they had all the advantages which were enumerated in the preceding chapter on their side,—unity of government, unity of language, religious, philosophical and social ideas which were permeating the whole Roman world, and adapting the soil for the reception of the new seed. It is significant that the cities which represented best the mixed character of Roman civilisation were just those which supplied the largest number of converts. Such was Antioch, such was Ephesus, such was Alexandria, such was the new city of Corinth, which Julius Cæsar had founded and Augustus established, such above all was Rome, the common centre in which all nationalities were at home. Had the missionaries taken the contrary direction and addressed themselves to the natives in the far east, they would have met with insuperable difficulties, and even if they had succeeded in one nation, they would have had to begin their work afresh in the next country to which they went.

(2) There was another reason which attracted Christian missionaries to the shores of the Mediterranean. The Jews had taken the same road before them, and the Acts of the Apostles inform us that Paul and his fellow-missioners always preached to the Jews first, and only turned in the second resort to the Gentiles. Very likely the Apostle made no formal rule of this kind, but there is every reason to suppose that the book of the Acts correctly states his actual practice. He could not well do otherwise. He argued from the Old Testament, and those who had no acquaintance with it could not possibly understand the reasoning of one who 'through the law 'had died to the law.' Indeed, we may assume without fear of serious error, that in Apostolic times even heathen

converts had either been formerly Jewish proselytes or had at least some knowledge of the Old Testament in the Greek translation. Thus the Jews of the dispersion prepared the way for Christianity, and helped to determine its geographical course, though they soon became its bitter enemies.

§ 2. The Jews in the Dispersion.

The Jews had spread from Palestine to Egypt and further Syria, thence to Asia Minor till they had their settlements in all the lands of the Mediterranean. As early as 140 B.C., the Jewish Sibyl boasts that 'the whole 'earth and sea were full' of Jews. Here, of course, allowance must be made for patriotic exaggeration, but the allusions in classical writers abundantly prove that the Jews formed an important and conspicuous element in the population of the Roman world.

(1) The Jews of the early Roman Empire were in one respect quite unlike the Jews of our own day. They had not yet displayed on any large scale their genius for finance. The Jews owed the wealth which they acquired at a later period to the prejudice of Christians; it was at a much later time than that with which we have to deal that the world, having become Christian, looked on loans at interest as criminal, and left open to the Jews a door which the Christians had closed against themselves. But the day of Jewish riches was still distant. Here and there wealthy Jews were to be found. There were princes like Herod Agrippa

I., who was the favourite of Caligula, and afterwards of Claudius; and ladies of rank like Berenice the Jewish beauty, whom Titus was on the point of marrying. Generally, however, cultivated society only thought of the Jews as of petty and squalid hucksters, who lived in low parts of the town, as of a hateful and contemptible race who obstinately separated themselves from their fellowmen, and were addicted to a foolish and lazy superstition. Their horror of pork, their Sabbath day, their circumcision, all made them the butt of Roman wit.

(2) Nevertheless, the Jewish religion was recognised by law, and the Emperors paid it official respect. They did everything to satisfy the Jews, provided that the Jews would show themselves loyal subjects. The Jews were not required to adore the genius of the Emperor. They were excused from appearing in a court of law on the Sabbath: if corn was distributed as a public dole on that day, the Jews could receive it on another day instead. They were not required to serve as soldiers. More than that, the Jewish community in a heathen town had formal authority to exercise civil jurisdiction over its members, and was even permitted to decide criminal cases and inflict corporal punishment within certain limits. Hadrian, for we need not consider the madness of Caligula, furnishes the only exception to this general toleration. After the Jewish rising of 133, he forbade the Jews to practise circumcision. However, this prohibition was withdrawn by the next Emperor, Antoninus Pius, so far as it applied to those who were Jews by birth. The law could not always save them from the fury of the people, who were irritated

by their strict Monotheism. But a Jew, who practised his religion peacefully, always had the Imperial authorities on his side. Christians sometimes professed the Jewish religion with the express object of securing the protection of the law.

(3) Judaism, despite the scoffs of literary men and the hatred of the people, made many converts during the first century and a half after Christ. Probably every western synagogue had its proselytes, while in great cities, especially in Rome, they were counted by thousands. Josephus tells us that the general public had long shown great interest in the Jewish religion: 'there is no town,' he adds, ' among Greeks or barbarians ' or anywhere else and no nation to which the observance ' of the Sabbath after our way has not penetrated, and ' in which the kindling of lights and many of our laws ' on food are not practised.'[1] This propaganda was due partly to that proselytising spirit which is so severely condemned in the gospel according to St. Matthew, and at which Horace laughs. But it was also due to the conditions of a time in quest of new faiths and rites, and particularly inclined to eastern religions. Judaism also owed much of its success to its intrinsic superiority. It was originally a tribal and afterwards a national religion: and it never ceased to be the religion of a race: it never had the heart to deliver its message to the world at large. Yet for a time it seemed to be on the point of doing so. The Jews, exiled in foreign lands, still held to the law. Some parts of the law, however, necessarily fell into disuse. They were far away from the temple, and so could not sacrifice. Most

[1] Josephus, *Against Apion*, ii. 40.

of them had no farm-land and no cattle; they could not therefore keep the law of tithes. Accordingly, they tended more and more to lay stress on Monotheism, on the moral parts of the law, on the purity of their family life. They were as yet content to use the Greek version of their Scriptures; even the prayers in the synagogue were said in Greek or Latin: the inscriptions on the tombs in Jewish cemeteries were for centuries after Christ written in Greek or Latin, not as now in Hebrew. They could boast of writers quick to adapt Greek philosophy and literature to the service of Jewish Monotheism. In short, Judaism all but promised to do what Christianity did, i.e. to supply the desideratum of a moral, rational, and universal, Monotheism. But from about the middle of the second century after Christ the legal and exclusive phase of Judaism obtained complete ascendancy. Far from seeking proselytes, the Rabbis declared that a proselyte was not to be trusted till the twenty-fifth generation. 'Day 'and night,' said a great rabbi, 'are required for 'meditation on the law, that hour which is neither 'day or night may be given to the profane writings 'of the Greeks.' In this way Judaism shrunk into its old limits, and Christianity took up the work which had dropped from the hands of the Jew. Meanwhile Judaism had been preparing the way for a daughter better able than she to conquer and to rule.

## § 3. The Spread of Christianity during the First Century.

The New Testament, and especially St. Paul's Epistles, supply much authentic and tolerably full information on the spread of Christianity in Apostolic times.

(1) The earliest evidence we have leads to the belief that the first disciples fled to their native Galilee when the crucifixion of their master plunged them into terror and dismay. It was there apparently that their faith and hope revived, there they were first convinced that Jesus lived, not in the shadowy world of the dead, but in heavenly glory. His spirit, as they thought, had come from heaven and appeared for brief moments to assure them of his victory over death and Hades. Full of this new confidence, they returned to Jerusalem, the holy city. Outwardly they were still Jews, observing the law and worshipping in the temple. But they were bound together and separated from other Jews by their common belief that the risen Jesus was the Messiah, that he had redeemed them by his death, and that he would soon come. again in the clouds of heaven to establish the kingdom of God. Even at Jerusalem there was a large admixture of Jews from the other countries of the Roman Empire, and we may well believe that such of them as became Christians promoted a liberal spirit among the disciples at Jerusalem, and had a sense, more or less definite, that the religion of Jesus was meant to be universal. Stephen, one of those Hellenistic or foreign Jews, is represented in the Acts of the Apostles as a champion of this larger and nobler thought, and though the speech attributed

to him is evidently the composition of the narrator, it may, and probably does represent Stephen's views. Be that as it may, Stephen's death and the persecution of the Christians which followed it, certainly promoted the spread of the Gospel in a wider area. The new teaching was proclaimed among the Samaritans, some of whom received it. It established itself on the coast of Palestine, not only in Joppa, but also in Cæsarea, a heathen town which had its circus and theatre, its temple dedicated to the worship of Cæsar and Rome, and in which Jews formed but a fraction of the population. The next stages were Phœnicia, Cyprus, and Antioch, which last was after Rome and Alexandria the most populous and magnificent city in the world. The mission at Antioch was, for more reasons than one, a turning-point in the history of the new church. The church at Antioch was not a colony from the mother church at Jerusalem. It was planted by men from 'Cyprus and Cyrene' on the north-eastern coast of Africa, by men whose names have perished, but who must have been Hellenistic Jews. Converts were made at Antioch from the heathen world, and this rather by force of circumstances than in virtue of any concerted plan. The new doctrine may have spread from the suburbs and poorer quarters of Antioch, till it reached the centre of the city with its Greek civilisation. Thus Christianity which had begun at Jerusalem was born again at Antioch, and for the first time manifested its independence of the Judaism from which it had sprung.

(2) One consequence of the change was that the outer world now recognised the disciples as a separate sect,

and gave them a name derived from the official title of the leader whom they followed. Just as the followers of Pompey or Herod were known as Pompeians or Herodians, so the followers of Christ were now called Christians. During Apostolic times the title was not, so far as we know, used by the Christians themselves. They spoke of each other as 'brethren,' 'believers,' and the like, while the Jews called them Nazarenes. But during the second century the title was accepted by those on whom it had been imposed, and has been cherished by them ever since. We may be sure that the name Christian was given by persons who did not understand that Christ was the Greek translation of the Hebrew word Messiah. They took the word Christ for a proper name, and when the disciples of the new faith adopted it, they too did so with little thought of their master's claims to be the Jewish Messiah. That point was invested with supreme interest for the first disciples: it held quite a subordinate place in the mind of the later church, recruited as it was from the Graeco-Roman world.

(3) A passing notice is all that can be given here to the great Apostle who strove to free Christianity from the limits of Judaism and to make it universal. He first attracted attention at Antioch, which was not far distant from his native Tarsus. Antioch was the starting-point of his first missionary journey. Thence he sailed to Cyprus, landed in Asia Minor and visited the cities of its southern coast. Afterwards he travelled further west, crossed to Europe and established churches at Philippi and Thessalonica, at Corinth, where he spent a year and a half, and perhaps at Athens. Later,

Ephesus was the centre of his work, and he died, as we shall see further on, at Rome. We know very little about the work of the earlier disciples who had lived with Jesus. We have the best possible evidence (that of St. Paul) for St. Peter's appearance at Antioch, and the tradition that he, like St. Paul, died at Rome, is accepted by many competent and independent scholars. The same may be said of another early tradition according to which St. John spent the closing years of his long life at Ephesus. The stories told about the rest of the twelve are in part contradictory and vague and are wholly worthless.

(4) What we know of Christianity during the time when the little band of the original disciples was dying out, is, briefly, this. It had its churches in Palestine, but Palestine a few years after St. Paul's death lost much of its hold on the Christian imagination. In A.D. 70 Jerusalem was stormed by Titus, the temple was burnt down, and the city became a heap of ruins. So it continued till in 136 A.D. or perhaps somewhat earlier Hadrian built on its site the new city of Ælia Capitolina, in which Jews were not even permitted to live. Beyond Palestine, Christianity had won firm foothold in Antioch, all along the coast of Asia Minor, and in some of the inland cities, in Macedonia, and in Greece. It had penetrated further south to Alexandria, where Mark the Evangelist is said to have preached, and further west to Rome, which after the fall of Jerusalem contained more Jews than any other city in the world. Antioch, Alexandria, and Rome, were then, as they continued to be long afterwards, the chief seats of the young church. No authentic tradition survives to tell us how or by whom

the gospel was first brought to the imperial city. It is certain that neither St. Peter or St. Paul can have founded the church, and we must be content with the conjecture that some Jewish proselyte to Christianity travelled to Rome, persuaded a few of his countrymen to believe in Jesus, and so laid the foundations of a church destined to exercise the most momentous influence on the fortunes of the world. St. Paul intended to visit Spain: that he really did so is scarcely possible, though the belief that he landed there can be traced to the latter part of the second century. It must be remembered also that the list of churches contemporary with the Apostles is apt, even when reduced to its real bounds, to convey an exaggerated impression. The churches may have been, and generally were, very small. So long as the presence of Christians did not stir the Jews to riotous assault, it was scarcely felt by the great heathen world. Think for example of the church at Corinth. Apparently all its members were able to meet in a single house, that of Gaius (*Rom.* xvi. 23). We have no statistics of the Pauline churches, and there is little advantage in conjecture based, *e.g.*, on the number of persons in the Ephesian church, whom St. Paul salutes in the last chapter of the epistle to the Romans. It has been thought that the number of St. Paul's converts in Asia, Macedonia, and Greece, did not exceed a thousand in all, nor is there any objection to this conjecture except that it is mere conjecture. Of these, as St. Paul tells us, not many were wise, not many were noble. Here and there, however, exceptions occurred. At Corinth, St. Paul counted Erastus, the treasurer of the city, among his converts. Before the first century ended, the Christian faith is said to have had adherents even in the imperial family. The evidence for this assertion does not reach absolute certainty, but it rests on arguments which raise it to a high degree of probability. We know from the historian Suetonius that two near relations of the Emperor Domitian were condemned by him. The one of these, Flavius Clemens, was according to Suetonius a man 'of despicable inactivity,' and another heathen historian tells us that he was put to death for 'atheism' and inclination to Jewish customs. His wife, Domitilla, also a near relation of the Emperor, was sent into banishment. So far the accounts correspond very well with the idea concerning Christians commonly held in the Roman world. A useless life without interest in public affairs, 'atheism,' or refusal to worship the gods of the state, were just the charges made against them, and to the end of the first century they were constantly confused with Jews or Jewish proselytes. Further, Eusebius, quoting a heathen historian who died about 220, expressly affirms that Domitilla was a Christian. Lastly, in modern times a cemetery has been discovered clearly intended for Christian burial, and an inscription bears record that it was given 'by the 'kindness of Domitilla, niece of the divine Vespasian.' It is situated near the cemetery in which the Roman bishops of the second and third centuries were buried.[1]

---

[1] Sueton. *Vit. Domitian.* 15. Dio Cassius in the epitome of Xiphilinus, lxvii. 14. Eusebius, *Eccl. Hist.* iii. 18.

## § 4. Advance in the next two Centuries.

The reader will see that the great centres of Christian influence during the first three centuries were already occupied during Apostolic times; in Antioch, Alexandria, Rome, the Christian cause was advancing and asserting its power beyond the limits of the local church. Further, the line along which Christianity was to travel had been determined, and even the extent of its future conquests was to some extent mapped out. During the remainder of our period, *i.e.*, in the second and third centuries, the church on the one hand enlarged her borders by pressing further west, and on the other occupied the territory in which she had placed her garrisons much more thoroughly. We may now proceed to sketch the geographical distribution of the church at the end of our period, noting the time and manner in which the most signal advances were effected. Once more, we shall follow the old route, beginning with the east and ending with the west.

(1) It has been said that Christianity made little progress in an eastern direction. To this, however, there is one notable exception. The Syrian city of Edessa, northeast of Antioch and east of the Euphrates, became a great seat of Christian teaching and of Christian literature. The legendary account of a correspondence between Jesus and Abgar, king of Edessa, is evidently fabulous, nor can any trust be placed in the story that Addai, said to have been one of the seventy disciples mentioned in the third gospel, laboured in Syria. However, as these legends took form at a very early time, they are proof

that the Syrian church had claims to great antiquity. We know that Tatian, a Christian Apologist, who, though a Greek by education, was born in Assyria, and was possibly of Syrian origin, laboured in the Syrian church. Somewhat later, towards the end of the second century, Abgar, prince of Edessa, was a Christian: Edessene coins of that time are stamped with the cross, and the chronicle of the city records the destruction of a Christian church by earthquake in 202. Moreover, about the same time, if not earlier, the greater part of the Old and New Testaments were translated by Christian hands into Syriac. This version is substantially the same as that which is used at this day by the Syrian Christians. The churches which now use it are but the shadow of a glory which was ruined by the Mohammedan conquests and has now departed. But the Syriac church was once powerful; it stretched far and wide; it had a considerable theological literature, and indirectly by the translation of Greek philosophical works rendered great service to the Arabs, and through them to western Europe. This, however, does not concern us here. For our present purpose it is more important to notice that Edessa was conquered by Trajan, so that we can scarcely reckon the church of Edessa an exception to the rule that the limits of the Roman Empire were the limits of Christianity. But there were Christian churches in the new Persian Empire which arose in 226, and the ruler of the greater Armenia (which was also independent of Rome) established Christianity as the national religion. Here the change from heathenism to Christianity began in 286. In that year Gregory, surnamed the Illuminator, returned from Cæsarea in Cappadocia. He had been carried thither by his nurse when his family was massacred.[1] He was brought up in the Christian faith and carried it back to his native land. Persuaded by his teaching, Tiridates III. erected churches and schools. The Armenian church had strong national characteristics. It always stood more or less apart, and was soon completely sundered from the church of the Roman Empire.

(2) Turning westward, we find Christianity pressing from the southern and western coasts into the interior of Asia Minor. Some additions also were made to the Christian congregations on the coast. Smyrna, the most imposing and wealthy town in Asia Minor, is never mentioned in the New Testament, except in the epistles to the seven churches at the beginning of the Apocalypse, which were probably written after the Apostolic age. Nothing, indeed, forbids us to suppose that some disciple of St. Paul, or even St. Paul himself, when Ephesus was his head-quarters, may have founded the church there. Certain it is that the church was well known in the second century, and the venerable form of the martyred Polycarp who presided over it, is among the most familiar in ecclesiastical history. On the north coast Christianity as early as the beginning of the second century threatened to take complete possession of Bithynia. In Pontus, where the coast bends to the north-east, the faith was revived, established, and greatly extended by Gregory the 'Wonder-worker' in the latter half of the third century. No detailed account of his labours can be given, for his life, as the name 'Wonder-worker' indicates, became the subject of the wildest and most incredible legends. But Gregory himself is

[1] It is said that he belonged to the royal house of Parthia.

a perfectly historical character, who has left authentic writings. There is no reason to doubt that he gave a Christian character to the country in which he took up his abode; and Neo-Cæsarea, of which he was bishop, became a place of mark in the universal church.

(3) Corinth continued to be the chief seat of Christianity in Greece, and one well-attested fact conveys some idea of the progress which Christianity had made in Greek lands. Eusebius tells us that Dionysius, who was bishop of Corinth under M. Aurelius, wrote to the churches of Athens and of Lacedæmon, and also to those in the island of Crete.[1]

(4) From Alexandria the church travelled up the banks of the Nile and permeated Egypt. At first the converts were supplied by the Jewish and Greek population, but native Egyptians also were added to them. For the version of the New Testament in the Sahidic dialect, *i.e.*, in the Coptic of Upper Egypt, is supposed to date from the third century after Christ, and we learn that there were Christian confessors in the Thebais during the persecution of Septimius Severus (193–211). Closely connected with Egypt was the fruitful province of Cyrenaica, which lay to the northwest along the southern shores of the Mediterranean, and is now known as Barca. It is not therefore surprising to find Christians there as early as the middle of the second century.

(5) In the west, Rome, the seat of empire, was also the capital of Christianity. We learn from a letter of Cornelius, bishop of Rome in the middle of the third century, that the church of the metropolis had a large

---

[1] Eusebius, *Eccl. Hist.* iv. 23.

staff of clergy, and maintained no less than 1500 indigent persons from the common funds.[1] We know nothing of the way in which Christianity spreads to the other cities of Italy and to those of Sicily. Worthless legends, embodied in the Roman Martyrology, attribute the foundation of many churches in these territories to St. Peter and his disciples. We have however authentic information that sixty bishops met at Rome in 251 A.D.,[2] though unfortunately we cannot tell the names of their sees. The bishops of Capua, Milan, and Aquileia, attended the council of Arles in 314.[3]

(6) The church in Proconsular Africa was an offshoot from that of Rome. Thence the faith spread along the northern coast of Africa to the adjoining provinces of Numidia and Mauretania. Here, as in so many other places, the precise time and circumstances in which Christianity was planted cannot be ascertained. When we first make acquaintance with the African church, we find it already vigorous and influential. Agrippinus, bishop of Carthage in the first twenty years of the third century, was able to convoke a synod of seventy African and Numidian bishops. 'We are of yesterday,' says Tertullian, not probably without rhetorical exaggeration, 'and we have filled your whole territory, cities and 'islands, fortresses and towns.'[4] Converts were made from all classes, even from men in dignified and official position;[5] and Tertullian tells Scapula the governor of Proconsular Africa that, if he means to destroy Christianity, he will have to kill every tenth man in Carthage,

---
[1] Eusebius, *Eccl. Hist.* vi. 43, 11.   [2] Eusebius, *Eccl. Hist.* vi. 43.
[3] Hefele's *Councils*. I. Ch. iii. § 15.
[4] Tertullian, *Apologeticus*, 37.   [5] *Apol.* 1.

the capital.[1] One fact, which rests on better evidence than the fiery rhetoric of Tertullian, gives special interest to African Christianity. It was the birth-place of the first Christian literature in the Latin tongue. The Roman church during the first two centuries was much more Greek than Roman. The Roman bishops bear Greek names, the earliest Roman liturgy was Greek, the few remains of Roman Christian literature are Greek. The Christian literature of Africa was written in Latin almost from the first, and in the person of Tertullian, Africa gave to the church of the Empire one of the only two writers of conspicuous genius which it possessed till the close of the third century. Through Tertullian, Africa has left its mark on the popular theology of the present day. Again a large majority of the scholars who have devoted themselves to the investigation of the subject believe that the first Latin version of the Bible was made in Africa. If this theory be correct, we have another instance of the way in which African Christianity has affected the modern world. For the Roman Catholic church still uses a version of the Psalms and of the New Testament, which, though subjected to the revision of St. Jerome, is yet identical in substance with that which originated in the early African church.

(7) The first churches in Gaul were daughters, not of Rome, but of Asia Minor, and maintained ties of close friendship with the east. Lyons and Vienne in Provence were apparently the oldest of the Gallic churches. Pothinus, bishop of Lyons who died a martyr in 177, and his successor Irenæus, both came from Smyrna. A letter describing the persecution of the Gallic Christians

[1] *To Scapula*, 5.

under Marcus Aurelius is addressed by the churches in Vienne and Lyons to 'the brethren in Asia and Phrygia.'[1] This letter, which is among the most precious remains of Christian antiquity, was written in Greek. Irenæus, the first of the Gallic Christians who made a name as an author, used the same language. It was slowly and with great difficulty that the church advanced northward and westward in Gaul. We have an authentic record of the martydom of Saturninus, bishop of Toulouse, in 250. According to Gregory of Tours seven missionaries came about this time from Rome and established the churches of Toulouse, Arles, Paris, &c. There may be some foundation for the story, which is not in itself unlikely. But Gregory of Tours is too late and too credulous an author to inspire much trust.

(7) Irenæus and Tertullian testify to the existence of the Spanish church in their own time, and it could hardly fail to arise at an early date, considering the constant intercourse between Spain and Italy. But we have no means of determining the progress which Christianity had made in the Spanish peninsula when they wrote. A council of bishops met at Elvira in Southern Spain at the beginning of the fourth century, and at that time there were Christian churches scattered throughout the whole extent of the country. Seville, Malaga, Cordova, Toledo, Merida, Leon, Saragossa, cities of southern, middle, and northern Spain, were all represented in the synod. Christianity had also established itself at the end of the third century in the cities of Romanised Germany, along the banks of the Rhine and the Moselle, *e.g.*, in Mayence and Treves, and

[1] Eusebius, *Eccl. Hist.* v. 1 seq.

in the Roman provinces which lay to the south of the Danube. Nowhere are the first beginnings of Christianity more utterly obscure than in the country which has most interest for us, viz., in Britain. In 314 we find the names of three British bishops appended to the acts of the synod of Arles. These were the bishops of York, then the capital of Britain, of London and of Caerleon.

It was not, as has been already said, till the latter part of the third century that Christianity struck root beyond the eastern boundaries of the Empire. The conversion of the northern barbarians followed much later, and during the first three centuries the work had not been begun on any great scale. True, if we believe Tertullian, there were places in Britain which had not been touched by the Romans, and which were nevertheless 'subject to Christ,'[1] and Irenæus speaks of 'many barbarous nations 'on whose hearts salvation had been written by the spirit 'without paper and ink.'[2] But such vague statements count for little, though it is credible enough that a few barbarians on the border-line of the Roman provinces were influenced by Christian teaching. But the conversion of a barbarian tribe must have affected its whole manner of life, and raised it to a higher degree of culture. Of any such change in any single case no sign or token appears in the history of the first three centuries.

---

[1] Tertullian, *Against the Jews*, 7.
[2] *Against Heresies*, iii. 4. 2.

## § 5. How Churches Began.

As we review the ground over which we have gone, we are struck by the mist which enshrouds the origin of the early churches. Yet this is only what might have been expected. In the early days of Christianity before the church was organised, it grew and spread on no fixed system, naturally and spontaneously. We are accustomed to think of missionaries as of persons who have been trained for their work, and are then sent forth to a definite sphere with the formal sanction of the church to which they belong. In the early church it was otherwise. Its apostles (and it must not be forgotten that both the name and office of an apostle outlived the times which we call apostolic) were in one sense missionaries. But they had no formal commission; they needed no human education; they sped hither and thither at the call of some vision of the night or of the spirit which spoke to their hearts. These apostles or wandering missionaries come prominently forward in an early work recently discovered, and known as the 'Teaching of the Apostles.' Much later, Eusebius refers to wandering teachers of the same kind, calling them, however, not apostles, but evangelists.[1] Add to this that Christianity must have been propagated by the brisk intercourse which was constantly bearing merchants, soldiers, slaves, from one part of the Empire to another. The commercial relations, e.g., between Asia Minor and Gaul, Italy and Spain, Italy and Africa, were such that it was impossible for Christianity to exist in one of these countries without

[1] *Teaching of the Apostles*, xi. Eusebius, *Eccl. Hist.* iii. 37, 2, 3.

crossing the sea and landing in the other. The disciples would meet in a house, or there might at the same time be independent gatherings in several houses of the same city. How impossible to fix the moment when the household meeting grew into a church! How easy to forget the name of him who first spoke about Jesus, about his teaching, his death and his resurrection, to those who till then had known none of these things. When we enquire about the founder of an early church, we may often be putting a question which is inapplicable. For many of the early churches were not founded, but grew.

### § 6. Numbers of the Christians.

In what proportion did the number of the Christians stand to the entire population of the Roman Empire?

Unhappily we have no means of giving anything like an exact or even an approximate answer to this question. A modern scholar has calculated the proportion of Christians to the entire population, when the last persecution was over and the first Christian Emperor reigned, as about one fifteenth in the west, and perhaps one tenth in the east. We have no data to justify this calculation. But we have abundant proof that heathenism was able to maintain a vigorous life for centuries after Christianity had become the religion of the state. Nor is there the least room for doubt that the Christians at the close of the third century formed no more than a small minority of the population. During the greater part of our period they attracted little attention from the world at large.

Tacitus and Suetonius show by their brief and contemptuous notice that they knew little about Christianity, and cared less. Epictetus and M. Aurelius dismiss it with a scornful phrase. A few writers had more to say on the subject; Lucian for example enlarges on Christian credulity, probably because it supplied an easy mark for his wit; and a few philosophic writers such as Celsus and Porphyry thought it worth their while to argue against Christian belief. But it is significant that Dio Cassius who lived under Alexander Severus (222-235 A.D.) and wrote the history of the Empire down to his own time, never once mentions the name of Christian. Of course, Christianity, like all other novelties, first became a power in the great cities. The word Pagan, which meant originally peasant, still testifies to the obstinate vitality of the old religions among the country people. Even here, however, there were exceptions, and that from early times. To this the younger Pliny is a witness beyond suspicion. He writes to Trajan in the year 112 that in the province of Pontus and Bithynia where he was governor, or at least in some part of it, the 'infection' of Christian superstition had invaded not only the cities, but also the small towns and country districts. It had come, he says, to such a pass that the temples were nearly deserted.[1] In Christian writers of the first, the second, and the third centuries we have passing allusions to the evangelisation of the country districts.[2] Moreover, small as the number of Christians may have been, they were constantly increasing in numbers and in confidence.

[1] Pliny, *Epp.* x. 96 and 97.
[2] Clement of Rome, *First Epistle*, i. 42; Justin, *First Apology*, 67; Origen, *Against Celsus*, iii. 9.

The older writers, indeed, did not think it possible that the Empire would ever become Christian, and looked for victory to the day when Christ would come to judge the world. But about the middle of the third century, Origen was confident that the time would come when of all religions that of Christ 'alone would prevail, since the 'Word was ever winning more souls.'[1] This was a bold and original view, first uttered, so far as can be known, by Origen himself.

A century before Origen's time the social position of Christian converts had undergone some change. They were no longer taken exclusively, or almost exclusively from the ranks of the poor and simple. Christian monuments in the Roman Catacombs confirm Tertullian's boast that men of rank found their way into the church. 'Rich people,' says Origen, 'some of those who hold 'places of dignity, delicate and noble ladies, welome the 'followers of the Word.'[2] With these came men of philosophic training, who, while they strengthened the Christian cause, profoundly modified the form and substance of Christian teaching.

[1] Origen, *Against Celsus*, viii. 68.
[2] *Against Celsus*, iii. 9.

# CHAPTER III.

## THE LEGAL POSITION OF CHRISTIANITY, AND THE PERSECUTIONS.

### § 1. General Antipathy to Christian Religion.

THE Christian church began its career in a world which had been prepared during a long time and in many ways for the reception of Christian teaching. When we consider how strong and how numerous these influences were, we naturally wonder that Christianity prevailed so slowly and never did embrace more than a fraction of the population, till it had enlisted the strong arm of Imperial authority on its side. The fact is that this wonder would be inexplicable were it not for our knowledge of counteracting causes. Christianity answered to many wants of the individual and of society, but it also provoked prejudice, contempt, and hatred. More than this, it seemed to offend, and to some extent it really did offend, that patriotic passion which burnt in the hearts of noble and enlightened men, during the best ages of the Roman Empire. It was for these reasons that the fate of the new religion appeared at first to be desperate and then to tremble in the balance. Looking back, we can see that the final issue was certain from the outset. Yet it was long before Christians dared to hope that the Roman world would submit to the yoke of Christ, long before the heathen adversaries felt any serious alarm.

(1) In one sense, as has been said, polytheism is tolerant. Neither the Roman public nor the Roman authorities cared to interfere with a man's belief. Nature-worships which have grown up in a dim past, nobody knows how, do not impose a creed, because they have no settled belief which can be stated in a creed. They are not theoretical, but practical. Certain rites are associated by immemorial custom with the welfare of the family, the tribe, the state. Sacrifice must be offered to the guardian divinities; the worship must be paid according to a prescribed ritual and sometimes in certain places and by persons specially qualified. Myths or stories about the gods arise, as attempts, more or less ingenious, to explain why it is that some particular mode of worship must be followed. The myth, however, is not the important point. The myths are later than the rites which they profess to explain; they varied from time to time and in different places; they had no canonical authority, for the Greeks and Romans had no sacred books. Therefore on the whole a Roman citizen, or the member of a subject state, might *think* as he pleased. He must not, however, *do* as he pleased. If he neglected the worship of the local deities, and—much more—if he was disrespectful to them in act or word, the god would be angry, and his curse would strike not only the immediate offender, but also those who tolerated him. Again each member of the

State was bound to promote its welfare by religious observance. He had no more right to abstain from the performance of his religious duties than to decline paying taxes. This was the view generally received in the Roman world and from the polytheistic stand-point no other view was either possible or conceivable.

(2) We can now understand the first charge popularly made against the Christians, the first reason which exposed them to bitter hatred. It was said that they were 'atheists,' and, strange as the accusation sounds to us, it was one which the populace could not help making. Here were people who had no altars, no temples, no sacrifice, and who absolutely refused to recognise the gods whom everybody else adored. To the outer world the spiritual worship of the Christians was simply unintelligible; their religion was no religion at all. Early Christian literature testifies to the constant repetition of this reproach. ' Away with the atheists,' was the cry of the mob when a Christian martyr was led to execution.[1] In public calamities, the people with fanatical fury demanded Christian blood. The Christian 'impiety' had drawn down divine vengeance, and there was no hope of relief till the anger of the gods was appeased by punishment of the malefactors. 'They 'think the Christians to blame for every public 'calamity, for every hurt that touches the people. 'If the Tiber rises to the walls, if the Nile does not 'rise over the fields, if the sky stands still [and does not 'fall in rain], if the earth moves, if there is famine or 'plague, immediately the shout is raised, "To the lions

[1] *Martyrdom of Polycarp*, 3.

'with the Christians."'[1] The position of the Christians was unique. Sometimes, indeed, Epicureans and Christians were associated in the popular mind, since both were supposed to contemn religion. But the irreligion of the Epicureans was less guilty and much less offensive. For they at least were ready when occasion offered, to take part in the public rites, and to yield outward respect to opinions which they did not hold.

(3) People so irreligious were thought capable of any crime, and this suspicion was aggravated by the secrecy of the Christian assemblies. It was reported and generally believed that the Christians availed themselves of the darkness of night to practise the deeds of darkness, to hold cannibal feasts and to indulge in the most horrible immorality. They were a 'sect which fled from the light and hid in holes,'[2] and this for most sufficient reasons. It was also believed that the Christians practised magic, and their faith was often described as a 'magical superstition,' an accusation which may have partly arisen from the fact that the Christians did claim to cast out demons and to heal diseases miraculously. As for the Christian worship itself, the wildest notions were entertained concerning it. Thus it was said that Christians worshipped the head of an ass,[3] an absurdity attributed in the first instance to the Jews. Tertullian mentions this strange belief of his heathen countrymen, and his statement has been confirmed by a discovery made in 1856. Excavations in the Palatine Mount at Rome brought to light a chamber which had been buried underground; a drawing made with some iron instrument on the stucco of the wall,

[1] Tertullian, *Apol.* 40, *Against the Nations* (i.e. Heathen) 1, 9.
[2] Minucius Felix, *Octavius*, 8.   [3] Tertullian, *Apologeticus*, 16.

represents a figure with human body and ass's head nailed to a cross, while a man stands below in the attitude of prayer. Still further the Greek inscription in rude but perfectly legible letters runs thus—'Alexamenos worships [his] god.'

(4) The feeling of the populace to the Christian communities was a mixture of contempt, horror, and dread. With the more educated classes contempt predominated. 'If a man be educated,' says Celsus, in mockery, 'let 'him keep clear of us Christians; we want no men of 'wisdom, no men of sense. We account all such as 'evil. No; but if there be one who is inexperienced, 'or stupid, or untaught, let him come with good heart.' 'They are weavers, shoemakers, fullers, illiterate clowns.' 'The greater part of you,' says Cæcilius, 'are worn with 'want, cold, toil, and famine; men collected from 'the lowest dregs of the people, ignorant, credulous 'women.'[1] These accounts of the class in society from which converts were made, had ceased to hold good at least as early as the beginning of the third century. But mockery on this score continued to pursue the Christians even after the establishment of the Christian religion by Constantine; and Julian, his reactionary successor, condescended to use the old weapon of ridicule. Accordingly, since, as was taken for granted, the Christians belonged to the lowest classes, their credulity excited no surprise, and their patient courage in suffering was set down as perverse obstinacy. This obstinacy was their characteristic offence in the eyes of cultivated men, such as the younger Pliny, Epictetus, and M. Aurelius.

[1] Newman's *Grammar of Assent*, p. 461, from which the last three translations are taken.

## § 2. Christianity Illegal.

If the Christians had merely made themselves hateful and contemptible, if they had merely aroused the suspicion of statesmen by the secrecy of their meetings and their withdrawal from public life, they might still have appealed to the protection of the Roman law. They themselves felt that they lived under a system of equal justice and not under the absolute sway of tyrants.[1] As it was, however, no appeal could be made to justice, and the only hope of the Christians lay in the mercy and humanity of their rulers. From the outset, Christianity lay under the ban of the Roman law. There was no need of new enactments, it had been condemned by anticipation in the very infancy of the Roman constitution.

(1) First, Christianity fell under the ban of the law, because it was a new religion. The ancient law of the Ten Tables thus formulated the prohibition of any such innovation—'Let no one have gods apart or worship new or 'strange gods privately, unless these gods be admitted 'by public authority.' This law applied to Roman citizens, for of course foreign subjects of Rome were allowed and expected to worship their national deities, nor was the prohibition in the case of Roman citizens absolute. The state, in time of war, plague, or the like, might adopt foreign worships, which were sanctioned by the college or board of Pontiffs. But a new worship meant the introduction of an agency too powerful for committal to private hands. Under the Empire this law became impracticable, but it was never repealed,

[1] Tertullian, *Apologeticus*, 2.

## WHY IT WAS ILLEGAL

and always lay ready for use against the Christians. The penalty, if the criminal belonged to the upper classes, consisted in banishment to an island: persons of humble station were liable to death. The practice of magic obviously included all the dangers attendant on the introduction of a new religion in an aggravated form, and was visited with the same penalties. The Romans called the wizard 'maleficus,' that is, 'the evil doer' by pre-eminence. On this count also the Christians were liable to prosecution, their religion being constantly associated with the black art in the public mind.

(2) Next, and this was a much more serious matter, Christians were liable to the penalties of sacrilege and high treason, of sacrilege for refusing to worship the gods of the state, of high treason for refusing to worship the genius of the Emperor in whom the majesty of the state was embodied, with the customary offerings of wine and incense. For these two kindred crimes the punishments were most severe. Persons of condition might be decapitated; the magistrate might sentence those of inferior station to death by burning, or by crucifixion, or he might have them flung to the wild beasts in the amphitheatre. Moreover, a Roman citizen accused of high treason might be put to the torture, a mode of question which in all other charges was reserved for slaves.

(3) Lastly, a Christian congregation with its frequent meetings, common funds, and social meals, was in the eyes of the law a club. Now clubs were forbidden and rigidly suppressed by the Imperial authorities. In a few cases the law was relaxed, the members of a trade were allowed to form themselves into a guild, and benefit clubs for the interment of the dead were permitted.

After a time, Christians availed themselves of the leave given to form burial clubs, and in this way they acquired property in land which they used ostensibly for burial of the dead, but also for secret religious meetings. It is to be observed, however, that the Roman magistrates in their nervous dread lest any club might be perverted for political purposes, required even industrial and burial clubs to ask the approval of government, which was only given on strict conditions. It is obvious that Christians could not justify before the courts associations which on the face of the matter were sacrilegious and treasonable.

### § 3. Varying Rigour of the Magistrates.

The execution of these laws rested at Rome with the Prefect of the city, and in the provinces with the governors. A good deal depended on the humour of the official in charge, on the temper of the people, and the disposition of the magistrate to pamper or control it. Hence penalties might be inflicted with varying severity in neighbouring provinces, and in the same province one governor might leave the Christians alone, while another might treat them according to the rigour of the law. Thus in Proconsular Africa, Scapula, who administered the government there about 211, persecuted the Christians with appalling barbarity: yet some of his predecessors in the same province had devised pretexts for letting the Christians escape, and at the very time when Scapula was torturing his Christian subjects, and exposing them to horrible deaths, the governors of Mauretania and of Leon in Spain simply beheaded obstinate Christians.[1] It must be added that bribery often obtained alleviation of their imprisonment, and even complete exemption for Christians.

(1) It has been thought strange that some of the best Emperors persecuted the Christians, while it was under some of the worst that the church lived in entire or comparative peace. There is, however, nothing surprising in this. A good Emperor like Trajan, M. Aurelius, or Decius, would feel bound to administer the law. He might wish to do so with all possible humanity: still, he would consider it his duty to see that the law was carried out. Moreover, patriotic Emperors, such as those just named, hated Christianity because they were patriotic. It seemed to undermine, nay, really did undermine, the foundations of the whole social fabric. How could they foresee that new and better order which was to arise under Christian influence from the ruins óf the older civilisation? The Christians themselves, as we have observed, had no presentiment during the first two centuries and a half of the church's history, that any new social order would arise. They only felt sure that the old order was doomed, and were not slow to express their conviction. On the other hand; a worthless tyrant might indeed glut his thirst for blood by persecuting Christians, but he might favour them from some personal caprice, and he would feel no obligation to execute the laws, unless personally inclined to do so. Thus the cruel and profligate Commodus gave their freedom to the Christian confessors who had

[1] Tertullian, *To Scapula*, 4.

been condemned to work in the Sardinian mines. He did so at the request of Marcia, his Christian mistress; 'the God-loving Marcia,' a contemporary Christian writer calls her.[1] Again, an Emperor whose blood and sympathies were Oriental rather than Roman, would be free from the genuine Roman aversion to the new and barbarous religion. Elagabalus and Philip the Arab are instances of worthless Emperors of eastern proclivities who favoured Christianity: we shall find Severus Alexander pursuing a like course from nobler and more reasonable motives. We must consider further that the disasters of the Empire and the fact that the men in power had their hands full, told in favour of the Christians. An Emperor who was occupied with intestine feuds, or with war against barbarian invaders, was apt to forget the Christians and to leave them alone.

(2) Nevertheless, the Christians held an unique position which could not fail to attract the lightning of Imperial vengeance. There were other new religions, and on the whole they were tolerated. Magicians were often tolerated in practice: so were some of the clubs which defied the law and honey-combed the Roman world. The peculiarity of the Christian position was that it united in itself so many different kinds of illegality, so many causes of popular hatred and distrust. The Christians stood alone—if we put aside the Jews, who were excused on hereditary grounds—in their obstinate refusal to recognise the worship of the State, which to the Roman mind was all one with the refusal to acknowledge the State itself. When the Christians were sufficiently numerous, they constrained attention chiefly by

[1] *Philosophumena*, ix. 12.

characteristics which were really honourable to them, but which were misunderstood; by that common love which overstepped all division of race and class, by their withdrawal from a world which 'lay in iniquity,' and sometimes also by a fanaticism which cannot be justified, though it admits of easy excuse. The belief that martyrdom gave immediate admission to heavenly glory, caused that feverish thirst for a martyr's death which is so prominent in the Ignatian epistles. The Puritanical rigorism of many Christians condemned even innocent participation in public rejoicings, and a Christian soldier under Septimius Severus died rather than wear a garland on his head, when he went before the tribune with the other soldiers to receive his pay. Some Christians held all flight from persecution to be unlawful, and occasionally fanatics brought death on themselves by a gratuitous profession of their faith before the tribunal of the magistrate, or by violent insults to the idols and the temples. It is only fair to say that the common sense of the Church reprobated these excesses.

§ 4. The Three Periods of Persecution.

The history of the persecutions falls naturally into three periods. During the first of these Christians were exposed to violence and injustice, but had not, so far as can be ascertained, been brought before the tribunals as the adherents of a new and unlawful religion. It extends from the beginning of Christianity to the reign of Trajan. The second period begins with the edict of

Trajan addressed to the younger Pliny in the year 112. That edict regulated the judicial procedure against persons accused of Christian superstition for about 150 years. The rule laid down was that Christians were not to be sought out, but that if they were brought before the tribunals and remained obstinate, they were to be punished according to law. A new era began with the reign of Decius (249-251.) This Emperor opened the series of general and systematic persecutions conducted by the State, with the deliberate design of exterminating the Christian religion. This third period closes with the year 313, in which the edict of Milan gave the Christians the legal right to exist. Thus, the reigns of Trajan and Decius constitute the great dividing lines. The characteristics of these eras will be explained further on more accurately and fully. Meantime, it may be well to warn the reader that the popular list of ten great persecutions has no historic worth, and is simply misleading. It first appears in St. Augustine and was probably fixed on some fanciful principle, e.g. that the ten persecutions answered to the ten plagues of Egypt, or the ten horns on the head of the beast in the Apocalypse.

## § 5. The First Period.

(1) It is plain from St. Paul's epistles, and from the Acts of the Apostles, that the Christians had much to suffer from the first. But it was not the Roman magistrate who was their enemy. He on the whole was their

protector: it was their Jewish countrymen who pursued them with implacable hatred, and occasionally contrived to excite the heathen populace. For a time, the Roman authorities, and the public in general, made little or no distinction between the Nazarenes and other Jews. Hence the complaint of the impostors at Philippi when St. Paul had exorcised the hysterical girl, and deprived her masters of the gain they made by her soothsaying: 'These men, being Jews, do exceedingly trouble our 'city, and set forth customs which it is not lawful for 'us to receive or to observe, being Romans.' Hence Gallio, the Proconsul at Antioch, is said to have treated the question between St. Paul and his opponents as a question of Jewish law, which need not trouble him. Hence, the Jews at Ephesus felt the need of putting forward Alexander as their spokesman, with the view of dissociating their cause from that of the new teaching, and from the odium which it had drawn upon itself. The same confusion underlies the famous but obscure statement of the Roman historian Suetonius.[1] He tells us that the Emperor Claudius ' drove out of Rome the 'Jews who were excited to constant riot by Chrestus.' We know from other sources that the heathen sometimes mistook the meaning of the title 'Christus,' (*i.e.* anointed) and pronounced or wrote it 'Chrestos' (*i.e.* 'good·' or 'simple.'[2]) Suetonius had apparently heard some dim and confused rumour of the disputes between the Roman Jews and the Roman Christians on the claims of Jesus to be the Christ or Messiah. It was on account of these riots that Claudius, in the latter part of his reign, expelled or, it may be, only intended to expel the Jews from

[1] Sueton. *Vit. Claud.* 25.   [2] Tertullian, *Apologeticus*, 3.

Rome. Clearly, Claudius, to judge from the words of Suetonius, drew no line of demarcation between Jews and Christians. The latter were still 'under the 'protection of a religion which was most distinguished 'and undoubtedly lawful.'[1] But on the other hand, they had to share in the disrepute and misfortunes of the Jews with whom they were associated.

(2) Under Nero, the stepson and successor of Claudius, the Christians for the first time take a distinct place in the history of the Roman world. Suetonius simply says, that 'the Christians, a class of people addicted 'to a new and magical superstition, were severely 'punished.'[2] Tacitus, who was eight or ten years old at the time of the persecution, and must therefore have grown up among those who had witnessed it, has left us a much fuller and more striking picture. In the year 64, the greater part of Rome was burnt down, and the suspicion gained ground that Nero himself was the guilty cause of the calamity. He was naturally anxious to divert the odium elsewhere, and he resolved to make the Christians the scape-goat of popular fury. It was necessary that he should make a clear distinction between Christians and Jews, for he was enslaved by the influence of Poppæa, a Jewish proselyte, who had already proved herself ready to protect the religion which she had embraced. Poppæa cannot have failed to know something of the Christians, and it has been conjectured that she actually suggested the accusation which Nero made against them. The course which things took, may be best told in the words of Tacitus.

[1] Tertullian, *Apologeticus,* 21.   [2] Sueton. *Vit. Neron.* 16.

Nero, to put an end to the common talk, imputed it to others, visiting with a refinement of punishment those detestable criminals who went by the name of Christians. The author of that denomination was Christus, who had been executed in Tiberius' time by the procurator, Pontius Pilate. This pestilent superstition, checked for a while, burst out again, not only throughout Judea, the first seat of the evil, but even throughout Rome, the centre both of confluence and outbreak of all that is atrocious and disgraceful from every quarter. First were arrested those who made no secret of their sect; and by this clue a vast multitude of others, convicted, not so much of firing the city, as of hatred to the human race. Mockery was added to death; clad in skins of beasts, they were torn to pieces by dogs; they were nailed up to crosses; they were made inflammable, so that when day failed, they might serve as lights. Hence, guilty as they were, and deserving of exemplary punishment, they excited compassion, as being destroyed, not for the public welfare, but from the cruelty of one man.[1]

(3) From this account it follows that Nero, though he persecuted Christians, made no direct attack on their religion. They were accused of arson in its worse form, but not of breaking the law against the introduction of a new religion. It follows next that the Christians, as early as 64 A.D., were known by that name to the Roman mob: the words of Tacitus are express on this point, and there is no reason to doubt his accuracy. Further, although public opinion did not support Nero in his atrocious accusation, and men even felt some little pity for the sufferers, it was generally believed that the Christians were capable of almost any enormity. They were guilty of 'hatred to the human race.' They did in fact look forward to the conflagration of the world, and by an easy process of reasoning, it was

[1] Tacitus, *Ann.* xv. 44.

taken for granted that they wished and were ready to promote the end which they expected. 'They threaten,' said their opponents, 'the whole earth and 'the universe, stars and all, with conflagration; they 'plot ruin.'[1] Of this general repute Nero took advantage. But the persecution was in the strictest sense local: it is only later legend which extended it beyond the precincts of Rome. It was also accidental: as yet, no general measure arraigned those who confessed the name of Christ. The persecution, however, had one momentous result, if, as is probably the case, St. Paul perished in it. It also served to secure that immortal infamy for the name of Nero which is strongly marked in the veiled and symbolical imagery of the Apocalypse attributed to John.

(4) The suspicious nature of Domitian led him to banish a certain number of Christians, and we have already discussed the reasons for believing that two members of the Imperial family were implicated in the charges made against the Christians.[2] Hegesippus,[3] who lived about fifty years after Domitian's death, tells a curious story about the Emperor and two grandsons of Jude the brother of Jesus. He says that Domitian examined two brothers who were descendants of Jude, for fear that their claim to spring from the royal house of Judah might make them dangerous politically. He found, however, that they were poor and horny-handed peasants, whose hopes of a Davidic kingdom lay in another world, not in this. Accordingly, he let them go in peace, so that they lived till the reign of Trajan

[1] Minucius Felix, *Octavius*, xi. 1.  [2] See page 40.
[3] Quoted by Eusebius, *Eccl. Hist.* iii. 20.

and 'presided over the churches.' Nothing can be built directly on a story which looks so apocryphal, but it shows that in the belief of Hegesippus, Domitian was little inclined to prosecute Christians as such. This opinion is confirmed by Tertullian; Domitian, he writes, 'who had a fraction of Nero's cruelty, had tried [to 'persecute] but readily, as accorded with the man's 'character, put a stop to the beginning which he 'had made.'[1] Nobody pretends that the next Emperor, Nerva, did the Christians any harm. Indeed, we learn that he forbade accusations of 'impiety' and 'Jewish ways' and so shielded Christians from charges which spite or avarice might have brought against them.

## § 6. The Second Period.

The persecution of Christianity in the proper sense of the word was inaugurated by Trajan, and he settled those legal relations between the new religion and the state which lasted from the beginning of the second century till the year 249.

(1) Trajan's edict was occasioned by a letter from the younger Pliny, who in 112 was administering the province of Bithynia and Pontus, as pro-prætor.

(a) He found his province overrun with the new sect. He tells his master Trajan what he had done. If Christians were brought before his tribunal, he required them to offer wine and incense before the image of the Emperor, and to curse Christ. If they complied, as

[1] Tertullian, *Apologeticus*, 5.

many did, he did not molest them further. If on the other hand, they confessed themselves Christians and were steadfast in their confession, he questioned them a second or a third time, threatening them with punishment: if they still refused to comply, he sent them to immediate execution, deeming that their obstinacy in any case deserved death. He made an exception of Roman citizens tainted with 'the same madness,' sending these for trial to Rome. Pliny also says that after putting two female slaves to the question by torture, he could discover no immorality on the part of the Christians; on the contrary, one object of their society seemed to be the promotion of pure and honest life. So far Pliny's measures had been attended with considerable success. The temples which had been all but deserted, were again thronged with worshippers, and the sacrificial victims which had become almost unsaleable, found purchasers. Moreover, Pliny's edict which gave effect to his sovereign's prohibition of clubs or societies, had produced its effect, for the Christians had in consequence desisted from their common meal. So much Pliny had done on his own judgment, for before this time he had never witnessed the trial of Christians. Considering therefore the number of lives at stake, he desired instructions from Rome.

(*b*) Trajan's answer is short and pointed. The Christians are not to be sought out: no anonymous charges against them are to be received, for this would be a 'precedent of the worst kind and unsuited to our age.' Even if accused in due order, and suspected of the Christian superstition, they are not to be troubled further if they will supplicate the gods. But in case of obstinate refusal, punishment was to be inflicted. The Emperor entirely approves of the course which Pliny had taken, so that capital punishment must be meant.

(c) The rescript was worthy at once of Trajan's humanity and patriotism; of his humanity, for it avoids hard measures, so far as was possible, and discountenances the odious trade of the informer; of his patriotism, for Trajan from his point of view could not tolerate a system which would have undermined the whole structure of Roman polity. It has been said that Trajan's letter inaugurated a new epoch. It was not that he changed the law; Christianity as we have seen, was implicitly condemned by laws far older than itself. But Trajan realised, and we have at least no record of any prior realisation, the exact relation in which Christianity stood to the law, and clearly laid down the proper method of procedure. The days when Christianity could shelter itself under the wing of Judaism had passed away. The persecution of Christians no longer needed popular misrepresentation or corrupt motives in the magistrate. The clamour against Christians could now take the form familiar in later persecutions, *Non licet esse vos*, ' the law does not permit 'you to exist.' We may be quite sure that Trajan, humane as he was, would have gone to work in sterner fashion, had he lived late enough to witness the alarming increase of the Christians in numbers and influence.

(2) Trajan died in 117; the reigns of Hadrian, Antoninus Pius, M. Aurelius, and Commodus, all of whom followed in peaceful and orderly succession, extend nearly to the end of the second century, *viz.*, to 193. Hadrian shewed himself in the earlier part of his reign a wise and humane ruler, he patronised philosophy and literature,

though in these respects he was a mere dilettante. He was half sceptic, half devotee, and never wholly serious, till the fanciful humours which were characteristic of him changed during the closing years of his life into settled gloom. To him the various phases of religion were an object of eager curiosity : in a letter which he wrote after a visit to Egypt he makes casual mention of Christianity, but he put it on the same level with the worship of Serapis, and believed that, for all their sanctimonious pretences, money was the true god, both of Egyptian priests and of Christian presbyters. 'This is the deity whom Christians and 'Jews, yes, and all nations worship.'[1] There is only one case of a well-authenticated martyrdom during his reign, and in a rescript to the proconsul of Asia Hadrian protected the Christians from vexatious charges, and insisted that their prosecution should be conducted in strict accordance with the law.

(3) We hear more of martyrdoms under Antoninus Pius. Merciful as this Emperor was, he could not always protect the Christians from the popular fury, aggravated as it was by the physical calamities, earthquakes, famines, and pestilence, which beset an Empire preserved by the wisdom of its ruler from the scourges of war and misrule. We have an example of the popular feeling in the martyrdom of Polycarp, the aged bishop of Smyrna, which is now generally thought to have happened in this reign. The federation of Asiatic towns was holding its annual festival at Smyrna, and eleven Christians (we do not know how the persecution began) had been killed by

---

[1] The text of the letter is given in Lightfoot's *Apostolic Fathers*, part II., vol. i. p. 464. It has been preserved by Vopiscus, *Vita Saturnini*, 8.

wild beasts in the amphitheatre, to the delight of the spectators. Then a cry arose, 'Away with the atheists. 'Let search be made for Polycarp.' Mounted police fetched him from his retreat in the country: when he refused to deny Christ, a savage howl arose from Jews and heathens, and as the sports were over, he was burnt alive, instead of being thrown to the lions. Here it is worth notice that Trajan's rules were transgressed. The accused man was sought out, and this, though no accusation had been made in regular and legal form.

Another story which rests on good evidence, lights up another side of the conflict between Christianity and heathenism. A woman being converted to Christianity refused to gratify her husband in his foul desires; and after vain endeavours to make him lead a better life, finally separated from him. In revenge, he accused her of being a Christian. The trial was deferred at her petition, in order that she might settle some private affairs. Meantime her husband turned upon her instructor and brought him before the court. The accused man confessed his faith and was executed. Two other men who remonstrated with the judge and avowed their Christianity, suffered with him. Justin, who tells the story, adds that he too expected a similar fate.[1]

(4) Under the next Emperor, M. Aurelius, Christian blood flowed more freely than at any other time during the whole course of the first two centuries.

(a) More causes than one predisposed M. Aurelius to severity. As a just ruler, he esteemed himself the minister of the law, which he was bound to execute. His patriotism, cast in the antique mould, must have made the new

[1] Justin, *Second Apology*, 2, 3.

religion hateful to him. Besides this, his tutor Fronto (and never was a more docile and reverent pupil than Marcus) believed and propagated the coarsest scandal against the Christians. Marcus himself could see nothing in the courage of their martyrs except 'sheer obstinacy.' Justin and his companions were put to death at Rome by order of the City Prefect, who was the trusted friend of Marcus, and under the very eyes of the Emperor. Again, Marcus was personally responsible for the persecution in the South of Gaul, recorded in a contemporary letter from the churches of Vienne and Lyons to 'the brethren in Asia and Phrygia.'[1] The persecution in these cities was so severe that no Christian could venture out of doors. No mercy was shown to extreme age, to youth, or to sex. The governor of the province, instead of checking the enraged multitude, commanded the Christians to be sought out, so that here we have another instance of advance beyond the measures enjoined by Trajan. The prisoners were cruelly tortured, and some were exposed to the wild beasts. The governor, however, finding that one of his prisoners was a Roman citizen, thought fit to consult the Emperor on the course to be adopted. Marcus wrote back, telling him that those who denied their Christianity were to be set free, that the others were to be executed. It is needless to say that the Imperial rescript was readily obeyed. The Christians, if Roman citizens, died by the sword, if not, by the wild beasts in the amphitheatre.

(*b*) The persecutions at Madaura and Scillis, or Scillita, in Africa, happened just after the death of M. Aurelius, and must be regarded as the continuation of his policy.

[1] The text is given by Eusebius, *Eccl. Hist.* v. 1, 2.

But when the cruel and worthless profligate Commodus was established in power, the 'favour of God,' so Eusebius puts it, 'sent peace to all the churches throughout the world.'[1] It was only for a brief space that Commodus endured the virtuous friends bequeathed him by his father. Their virtues would have been dangerous to the Christians; afterwards the influence of Marcia was supreme, and the Church was safe. A Christian presbyter had been her foster-father; she was in communication with Victor, then bishop of Rome, and powerfully seconded his petitions. It is no doubt of Marcia and her protegés that Irenæus is thinking, when he speaks of 'the faithful who are in the Imperial court.'[2]

(5) From the death of Commodus in 193 to that of Philip the Arabian in 249, the Roman Empire underwent a change of condition.

(a) In the first place, whereas till that time the Senate had at least enjoyed great nominal authority, Septimius Severus began a military despotism, which was the rule thenceforth. 'Enrich the army, despise the rest,' are words attributed to him, and which are at any rate a good summary of his policy. Again, although Septimius Severus was himself born in the Latinised province of Africa, belonged to a good family of Roman knights, and had been admitted to the Senate by Marcus Aurelius, he married a Syrian; the political consequences of this marriage were important. The descendants of Septimius Severus, Elagabalus and Alexander Severus, were Oriental in their habits and views. So, as his name shows, was Philip the Arab, though he did not belong to the dynasty

[1] Eusebius, *Eccl. Hist.* v. 21.
[2] Irenæus, *Against Heresies*, iv. 30, 1.

of Severus. It was a new thing for the Romans to be governed by rulers who were Roman neither by birth or education. A Spaniard or a Gaul could scarcely be distinguished from a native of Rome itself: it was quite otherwise with a Syrian or an Arab.

(*b*) Probably both these changes, certainly the latter, affected the fortunes of the Christian church. Under Septimius Severus the Christians suffered more than they had ever suffered before, even under Marcus Aurelius. For a time, Septimius showed no personal hostility to the Christians. On the contrary, Tertullian assures us that, far from harassing 'most illustrious men, and most 'illustrious women,' of whose attachment to the Christian religion he was quite aware, he honoured them with his approval and openly withstood the fury of the mob.[1] Nevertheless, Septimius was an absolute sovereign, and he had much to do with the labours of the lawyers who elaborated the theory of absolute rule. He made Papinian prefect of the Prætorian guards: Ulpian and Paulus were his intimate friends. Now the fact that Christians stood beyond the protection of the law had been clear, ever since the time of Trajan. It is significant that Ulpian, in his treatise 'De Proconsule,' ('concerning the [duties of] a Proconsul') collected all the Imperial ordinances relating to the Christians. Under such circumstances we cannot be surprised to learn that the persecution was severe in Egypt and in Africa. Popular violence which appears to have been then at its height, might be disapproved at the court, but a governor was perfectly safe in enforcing the law, which was hard enough. In the tenth year of his

[1] Tertullian, *To Scapula*, 4.

reign, (the earliest years had been occupied with civil war) Septimius took a new step. 'He forbade conversion 'to Judaism under heavy penalty, and passed the same 'law concerning Christians.' This enactment in its letter left matters just as they had been since Trajan's reign. The same may be said of an enactment against 'illicit clubs.' But they betray the Emperor's disposition; they deprived the Christians of their best hope, *viz.*, that of escaping attention. Special irritation was caused by the refusal of the Christians to offer sacrifice to the genius of the Emperor, and even to take part in public rejoicings, which might have been thought innocent. Septimius had waded to the throne through blood: he had been engaged in a struggle for power and life, and for the unity of the Empire against two formidable rivals. In a time when great stress was necessarily put upon loyalty, the Christians were conspicuous as ' enemies of the Roman princes.'[1]

(6) Septimius, if he differed at all from his predecessors, only differed in this, that he was somewhat more resolute than any of them in his hostility to the Christian name. But the Emperors of eastern origin, on the contrary, displayed a friendly feeling to Christianity which was utterly unprecedented.

(*a*) Under Caracalla, the son of Septimius, and one of the worst rulers the world ever saw, the Church had peace, at least shortly after he had begun to reign. But Elagabalus, the effeminate fanatic who as Emperor still considered the worship of the sun-god, whose priest he had been at Emesa, the one serious business of his life, showed a positive liking to Christianity. For Roman statesmanship and for Roman religion he cared nothing,

[1] Tertullian, *Apologeticus*, 35.

and he did his utmost to make the worship of the sun-god, to whom he attributed his elevation, dominant at Rome. He wished all the religions of the earth to be absorbed in this one worship, and being most familiar with the cults of western Asia, he wished to treat the Jewish, the Samaritan, and Christian, religions as forms of sun-worship. Elagabalus represented the syncretism or mixture of religions, which had long been fashionable, in its most irrational and degraded form.

(b) His cousin, Severus Alexander, adopted a nobler type of the same tendency. In the brief but pregnant words of an ancient historian 'he suffered the Christians 'to exist.' He did more than this. He placed the image of Christ in his oratory, along with those of Abraham and Orpheus. When a Christian church disputed the possession of a piece of land with the guild of cooks, he decided in favour of the former. He gave as his reason that 'it was better for God to be 'worshipped, whatever the manner of worship might be, 'than that the land should be given to cooks,' a reason which makes his monotheism clear, if it throws some doubt on his sense of law and justice. He was attracted by the ethics of Christianity, and used to quote moral maxims of Jesus. A remarkable passage in Eusebius describes the relations of the Emperor's mother to a great Christian teacher. 'The Emperor's mother, whose 'name was Mammæa, a woman of extraordinary piety 'and circumspect life, when the fame of Origen had 'been noised abroad in all directions, till it reached her 'ears too, became very anxious to obtain a sight of the 'man, and to make proof of that knowledge which he 'had in divine things and which everybody admired. So 'when she was staying at Antioch, she sent a body of 'guards to invite him to her presence. Having spent 'some time with her, and having discoursed largely on 'the glory of the Lord and the virtue of the divine 'teaching, he hastened to his customary pursuits.'[1] Origen was also in correspondence with Philip, the Arab, who was the son of a Bedouin sheikh and became Emperor in 244. Eusebius mentions a letter written by Origen to him and another to his wife Severa.[2] An opinion gained ground from very early times that both Alexander and Philip had embraced Christianity, for when Dionysius, bishop of Alexandria, their contemporary, mentions Emperors who 'are said to have 'made open profession of Christianity,' the allusion can only be to them. The report is probably an exaggeration of the truth. Philip, if a convert at all, was one of whom the Christians had little reason to be proud.

§ 7. The Third Period.

We have found Emperors tolerant and more than tolerant to Christianity, but they left the laws which made it illegal, unchanged. In contrast to them, we have seen Emperors pursuing rigorous measures against their Christian subjects, but the persecutions were local and irregular : a few were put to death here and there, and from time to time, but there was no general persecu-

[1] Eusebius, *Eccl. Hist.* vi. 21.
[2] Eusebius, *Eccl. Hist.* vi. 36.

tion. Origen sums up the results in these words. 'It is 'very easy to count those who have died for the Christian 'religion; they are few and suffered on special occasions.'[1]

(1) A great change began under Decius (A.D. 249-251). He made the persecution systematic, and so opened a new period in the relations between the Church and the Empire.

(*a*) Previously the rule had been that a Christian when accused, should deny his Christianity, or pay the forfeit with his life. But Decius ordained that all Christians should be required to take part in the religious ceremonies of the state, and the magistrates were threatened with heavy penalties if they neglected to enforce the law. This was a formal departure from the course recommended by Trajan and followed by his successors. The first step was no longer left to private informers, for the duty of searching for Christians devolved on the officials of the Empire. The regulations were too precise to admit of any evasion. The Christians in each locality were to be summoned and required to sacrifice within stated limits of time. If they fled, they lost their property and their civic rights, and were forbidden, under pain of death, to return to their former home. Those who met the trial were dealt with according to a graduated scale of severity: by imprisonment, by the rack, by the pains of hunger and thirst, they were tempted to apostasy. Further a distinction was made between laymen and clerics, presbyters and bishops being put to death at once, unless they recanted.

(*b*) This change of procedure, striking as it is, is not hard to explain. Decius was a man of lofty virtue: he was a brave soldier, a skilful general, an able statesman,

---

[1] Origen, *Against Celsus*, iii. 8.

and the old religion seldom found a nobler champion than he. Unfortunately, he indulged in romantic delusions : he set his heart on restoring the enfeebled State by reviving Roman virtue in its antique severity. Instead of bearing himself as a military despot, he showed the utmost deference to the senate, and invited its members to choose a fit person for the obsolete office of censor. He who was chosen for the office by the acclamation of the senators acknowledged that the corruption of the times was beyond cure by such antiquarian expedients, but the Emperor persisted in his project. Manifestly, the Christians presented the first and most absolute obstacle to one who would fain have built up the state on its old foundations of Roman virtue and religion. The Christians were hateful to Decius for another reason. The barbarians were threatening the Empire, and, in a little, Decius was to die on the battle-field against the Goths. His one hope lay in presenting a united front to the foe, but internal union seemed impossible, if Christianity continued to exist. In this way Decius was forced into conflict with Christianity, and he saw (how could he help seeing?) that half-hearted measures were out of the question. The notorious increase of Christianity in number of adherents and influence would have made the measures which Trajan thought suitable, simply ludicrous. · If Christianity was to die at all, plainly it would die hard.

(2) The new mode of persecution produced new effects upon the Christians. They had never felt the weight of the Roman power before : their moral strength had been impaired by a long period of peace, and the trial came upon them when they had almost forgotten the sword which hung all the time over their heads. But a year

before, they had lived under a ruler who was said to be almost a Christian. Terror induced crowds to forswear Christianity: they pressed forward to the tribunals and purged themselves at once from all suspicion of Christianity. Others, by a strange device, contrived to appease their consciences without endangering their lives. They did not really offer sacrifice, but secured by a bribe an official certificate that they had satisfied the law. The casuistry of the church distinguished different degrees of guilt. There were some who countersigned the certificate with their own hands: others simply received it, while the least culpable merely allowed the statement of their compliance to be recorded in their favour by the courts of law. The authorities of the church had to decide in what way those who repented of their complete or partial apostasy were to be received. The problem occasioned much difficulty and dispute. It was a novel and curious spectacle which the world witnessed. Two highly organised powers stood over against each other. Each had its own laws: each enforced these laws by graduated pains and penalties. Between the two, there could be no lasting peace, or even mutual understanding. It was a struggle for life or death.

(3) Decius only reigned for two years, but the persecution which he began, was continued by Gallus, his immediate successor, and after a considerable pause by Valerian—from 257 to 260. Valerian, who had been promoted under Decius to the honourable but impossible office of censor, might have been expected to share the prejudices of Decius against the Christians. For a time, however, Valerian is said on very good authority[1] to have

[1] That of Dionysius of Alexandria, quoted by Eusebius, *Eccl. Hist.* vii. 10.

been kindly disposed towards them, and he only began the persecution when instigated by his favourite, Macrianus, an enthusiastic devotee of Egyptian sorcery. But, having put his hand to the work, Valerian followed that systematic method of which Decius had first set the example. Indeed, at the pass to which things had come, no other way could be thought of. In his first edict, he made it a capital offence to attend meetings for Christian worship, and in particular to visit the cemeteries which were habitually used for this purpose. All such places were confiscated by the state, and the Christians were required to 'recognise the Roman ceremonies.'[1] A second edict was issued with the design of separating the clergy from their flocks, and of putting a stop to conversions among the higher classes. 'Valerian wrote to the senate that bishops, 'presbyters, and deacons were to be punished in a 'summary manner [possibly by decapitation], that 'senators, persons of rank, and Roman knights, besides 'being degraded, were to forfeit their goods, and if after 'loss of their goods they continued Christians, to suffer 'death: matrons, after deprivation of their property, 'were to be driven into exile. Officers of the imperial 'court who had at some former time confessed them-'selves Christians, or did so now, were to forfeit 'their goods, to be put in chains and sent in detachments 'to the Imperial domains.'[2] The calm tone of this edict gives a very imperfect idea of the suffering inflicted. The Egyptian Christians in particular were sorely tried. Men and women, youths and maidens, were put to the proof by the rack and by severe im-

[1] *Act. Proconsulat. Cyprian*, i.  [2] Cyprian, *Letters*, 80.

prisonment. Death by decapitation must often have been welcomed as a relief.

(4) The systematic persecution which had continued with intervals from 250 to 260 failed, and it was followed by forty years of peace. The peace was not absolute: it is possible, and even probable that an occasional martyrdom occurred, for there was no repeal of the laws. Still, during these forty years there was no general persecution : Aurelian, it is true, intended to follow in the steps of Decius, but he died before he could give effect to his resolution. On the other hand, Gallienus (260-268) practically acknowledged the right of the Christians to form corporations and hold property. He wrote to several bishops, declaring his wish that they should not be disturbed, and restoring to the churches the buildings and lands which had been taken from them. Historians have gone too far when they have attributed to Gallienus the express and public toleration of Christianity. It was one thing to let Christian corporations hold land or buildings: the same privilege had been extended to other guilds, if licensed by the magistrates. It was another thing to annul the laws against Christian 'impiety,' and this last Gallienus did not do. Nevertheless he made it quite clear that he did not mean to execute these laws. It was no easy matter to interfere with the Christians, and the Emperor, in the disastrous times which followed the death of Aurelian, had quite enough to do without undertaking this troublesome business. A significant change also had taken place in the feelings of the heathen populace. In the early persecutions it was the mob which forced the magistrates to persecute: from the middle of the second century we find indications of popular sympathy with the Christians. When

Cyprian, bishop of Carthage, was put to death in 258, the heathen who had witnessed his charity during the plague, mourned for his loss,[1] and the martyrdom of a Spanish Bishop, Fructuosus, of Tarragona, which happened in the following year, awoke the same general compassion.[2]

(5) At the beginning of the fourth century, the Roman state made its last attempt to stamp out Christianity. This final conflict was the most severe of all.

(*a*) The Roman Empire had entered on a new lease of life. The long period of civil strife and humiliation at the hands of Persians and Goths was over for a season, and Diocletian, who began to reign in 284, was a vigorous and able statesman. He was the son of Dalmatian slaves, and for the old Roman traditions, or such fragments of them as survived, he had little reverence. He moved the seat of Empire from Rome to Nicomedia, on the shores of the sea of Marmora: he surrounded himself with oriental pomp, and guarded his sacred presence from the vulgar gaze: he took the title of 'dominus' or 'lord,' one which has descended to modern sovereigns, but which was utterly unknown in the days of the older Empire. But his was no idle ostentation. He set himself the serious task of restoring the Empire to safety and strength, and fell upon the plan of dividing it between several rulers, all, however, subject to his own ascendancy, and bound to act in concert. The scheme was supposed to provide for the defence of an Empire assailed on more than one side, for its diverse interests and for its unity. Diocletian,

[1] This appears from the Life of Cyprian by his deacon Pontianus, chap. 15.
[2] Ruinart. *Act. Martyrum*, Passio Fructuos. Episc. 3.

who was intensely superstitious, looked devoutly for the help of the gods in his great project. His name, Diocles, afterwards lengthened into Diocletian, was to him an omen that his glory would be under the guardianship of Zeus, and he did not forget that a Druidess had foretold his future greatness. He was also attracted by Neoplatonism, with its endeavours to mould all forms of heathenism into one, and quicken old religion with new life. Yet, notwithstanding the augurs and priests who attended him, Diocletian was for a long time tolerant to Christianity. Many of his courtiers were Christians; even his wife and daughter, it is said, were half inclined to adopt the new faith.

(*b*) Several causes contributed to bring on the critical struggle. It seems that he wished to erect a kind of heathen church in which the hierarchy of priests was to support the throne. Here the great Christian body stood in the way, and as the family of Constantius, one of the two Cæsars, or subordinate Emperors, already showed dispositions favourable to Christianity, the priests may have felt that their power was in danger, unless they could induce Diocletian to strike the first blow. They found it hard to do so, but in the end Diocletian's hesitation was overcome by Galerius, a rough and ignorant soldier, whose talents had raised him to the position of Cæsar. Galerius was as superstitious as Diocletian, his master: his temper was not trained and schooled like Diocletian's by education and political prudence: and he was specially devoted to the ancient rites of the Roman state. When the persecution broke out in 303, the Empire was divided thus: Diocletian, with the title of Augustus, reserved to himself Thrace,

Egypt, and the rich countries of Asia. Immediately associated with him was the Cæsar Galerius, who was stationed on the banks of the Danube with the care of the Illyrian provinces. Italy and Africa were consigned to Maximian, who, like Diocletian, bore the title of Augustus, while his Cæsar, Constantius Chlorus, governed Gaul and Britain. Each Cæsar married the daughter of the Emperor under whom he held his power, thus cementing political by domestic union. It was only the administration which was divided, for the ascendancy of Diocletian provided that the general policy of the Empire should be directed in concert. These political arrangements had an important bearing on the extent and relative intensity of the persecution.

(6) For some time previously, there had been signs of the coming storm. The numerous Christians in the army found themselves in difficulties which were indeed sometimes the result of their own indiscretion, but which were sometimes inevitable. Galerius peremptorily required Christian soldiers who were subject to him to sacrifice or to leave the army, and his power in the Empire and his influence over Diocletian were increased by his brilliant campaign against the Persians in 297. Still Diocletian hesitated. He took for granted that everyone should conform to the established religion, and as early as 296, in a decree against the sect of Manichees, had clearly stated the old principle that it was 'criminal in the highest degree to reopen questions 'settled and defined by the ancients.' But he had no wish to shed blood and begin a contest which must needs be long and difficult. At last, the importunity of Galerius, the counsels of augurs and soothsayers, who

deprecated the magical influence exercised by the sign of the cross, and Diocletian's own superstition, outweighed all other considerations. On the twenty-third of February, 303, the signal was given for a general and systematic persecution. It was the feast of the god Terminus, the god, who, as the legend told, had in the infancy of the Roman state refused to allow his removal to a new temple, and had so given the happy omen that no foe would ever move or contract the boundaries of Roman dominion. The Emperors Diocletian and Galerius were both in Nicomedia. Early on the morning of the feast, the chief church of Nicomedia, a magnificent building, was plundered and destroyed. Next day an Imperial edict was posted on the city walls. It comprised the following regulations :

All churches were to be destroyed, and the sacred books of the Christians burnt. Christians were to forfeit all civil rights. If injured, *e.g.*, by assault or robbery, they could claim no legal redress; much less could they hold any office under the state. Christians of humble station, if obstinate in their religion, were to be enslaved. Christian slaves were made incapable of freedom.

The real violence of a Christian who tore down this edict, the false rumours which attributed fires in the palace and petty tumults in Armenia and Syria, to the Christians, irritated Diocletian still further. Accordingly, a second edict condemned all Christian bishops, presbyters, and deacons, to imprisonment; a third edict ordered that the imprisoned clerics should be tortured with the utmost severity, till they consented to sacrifice. In 304, a fourth edict extended this law to all the Christians of the Empire.

## PERSECUTION BY DIOCLETIAN

(7) The duration of the persecution has been usually reckoned at ten years, *i.e.*, from 303, when Diocletian published his first edict against the Christians, till 313, when the edict of Milan established religious liberty.

(*a*) In fact, however, the general persecution did not last nearly so long. From 303 till the middle of 305, the Christians were everywhere persecuted, though even then the persecution was not severe throughout the whole of the west. Constantius, who ruled in Britain, Spain, and Gaul, had no inclination to persecute. He was obliged to treat Diocletian's edict with outward deference, and he was unable to prevent bloodshed in Spain, but in Gaul and Britain he simply deprived the Christians of their churches, and saved them, with rare exceptions, from further wrong. In 305, Diocletian, with his colleague Maximian, retired into private life, the structure contrived by Diocletian's skill fell to pieces, and the Empire was torn by intestine strife.

(*b*) The general character of the persecution ceased with the unity of the Empire. Constantius and his son relieved the Christians of all annoyance in Britain, Gaul, and Spain. The tyrant Maxentius, who reigned from 306 to 311, did the same good office for the Christians in Italy and (after 307) in Africa. About the same time, Licinius took the reins of government in Pannonia, Dalmatia, and Noricum, and the Christians there escaped further molestation. They fared differently in the East. All the Asiatic provinces besides Moesia, Thrace, Greece in Europe, and Egypt in Africa, were subject to Galerius and his nephew, Maximin Daza. In this vast territory things became worse instead of better. Galerius, who had been the original cause of the persecution, was no longer restrained by Diocletian, and went to work with redoubled energy. He inflicted death by slow fire on obstinate Christians, and his nephew, Maximin Daza, was as brutal and bloodthirsty as himself. There was no lack of apostasy, and the discipline of the church had to deal with a new class of delinquents, *viz.*, that of the 'Traditores,' persons who had surrendered the Christian Scriptures to the heathen magistrate.

(8) But there was no prospect of annihilating Christianity. Galerius and Maximin substituted mutilation and penal servitude for the penalty of death, and at last, in 311, Galerius confessed that his efforts had been useless, and in his 'clemency permitted the obstinate 'Christians to become Christians again, and to build 'churches, on condition that they respected public 'order.'[1] Galerius was in the agonies of disease when he dictated this decree, and he died a few days after its publication in Nicomedia. It was signed not only by Galerius, but also by Constantine and Licinius. The persecution was revived and continued, though with intermission and with less severity, by Maximin Daza, who succeeded Galerius in the government of the eastern provinces. Maximin died in 313, and the edict of Milan, published earlier in the same year by Constantine and Licinius, obtained the force of law in the east as well as in the west. This second edict of toleration adopted a much more respectful tone to Christianity, and sanctioned religious liberty in the widest sense of the word. 'Christians and all [other] 'men were to have free power of following their religion.'

[1] The text of the edict is given by Lactantius, *De Morte Persecutor*, 33, 34.

## ITS FINAL RECOGNITION

There was no restriction: 'each was to have unrestrained 'liberty in worshipping whatsoever he chose.' Church goods were to be restored to 'the Christian corporation,' *i.e.*, to ecclesiastics, not to private persons.[1] Henceforth, Christianity was secured in its claim to be a 'lawful religion.' Attempts to harass Christians in the exercise of their worship still occurred: even Licinius was tempted by political motives to transgress in an underhand and half-hearted manner the law of toleration which he had signed. But no general or systematic persecution ever occurred again. In 324, Constantine reigned alone over the whole Empire, and Christians found in him not only a protector, but a patron and benefactor.

### § 8. The Peace of the Church.

The edicts of toleration were welcome to the public as a whole, whether Christian or heathen. People were weary of bloodshed. The sympathy which the heathen had shown with Christian martyrs in the persecution of Decius, was evinced much more decidedly in that of Diocletian. Athanasius[2] had heard old men tell how at Alexandria, many heathen had given Christians a refuge in their houses, and had suffered fine and imprisonment rather than betray them. But welcome as they were, edicts of mere toleration were but for a time. The language of the edict of Milan sounds strangely modern. It might have been written by an English

[1] Lactantius, 48.  [2] Athanasius, *Ad Monachos*, 64.

or French 'philosopher' during the last century. For this very reason it was a mere makeshift, which had no chance of lasting in the fourth century. It was not possible, as yet, to conceive of a state which took a position of impartial indifference to all religions. How could the Empire prosper, if it was not hallowed and sanctioned by sacred rites? How could the magistrate hold himself aloof, when the cause of religion was at stake? Christians had indeed pleaded without conscious dishonesty for freedom of conscience, when that was the most they could hope for. In reality, nobody believed in the rights of conscience, the Christians least of all. They would have counted it disloyalty to the truth, and we must remember to their credit that they had been the sole champions of truth and adherence to it against custom and outward conformity. Constantine had set the Christians free from a law which required them to sacrifice under pain of death. Constantine's son and successor, Constantius, made heathen sacrifice a capital offence, and thus exactly reversed the positions of the two religions.

# CHAPTER IV.

## THE LEARNED DEFENCE OF CHRISTIANITY.

### § 1. Changes in the Second Century.

THE title of this chapter might convey the impression that Christianity, or at all events the Christianity of the first three centuries, was a definite system, rejected and attacked by some, embraced and defended by others, a system which during the time mentioned underwent no radical change, and which could be easily understood by friend and foe, if they took the pains to study the question. The same conception may seem to underlie the previous chapters also. We have spoken of the extent to which Christianity spread, and of the persecutions which assailed it, as if Christianity had all the time continued one and the same. The language used has its sufficient excuse in convenience and indeed in necessity. Nor is it without adequate justification in the reason of the thing. There is a degree of unity which links together the Christianity of all ages and of all kinds: probably no set of so-called Christians has entirely passed beyond the formative power of the few mighty principles which Jesus stated with unique purity and force. So far Christianity is one.

(1) It is, however, no less true that Christianity has been in constant flux, and never has it changed more rapidly and deeply than in the first three centuries of its existence. So clear is this that even learned Roman Catholics, bound as they are to the theory of an unchangeable church, have practically shifted their ground, and now admit that Catholic doctrine has gradually developed or grown. In fact the change is much more vital. At first there was no Church at all in the modern sense of the term. There were many local churches, and there was one Church throughout the Roman world—because the members of the particular congregations believed in one God— aimed at holy living, acknowledged Jesus as their master, shared the common hope in the coming of the Lord, and so looked forward to a time, and that not far distant, when the kingdom of God founded by Jesus would be set up in power. But if we mean by the universal Church a corporate body with an external government and constitution of its own, then of such a body there is no trace during the first 150 years of the Christian era. After that time the Church was on the way to external unity, attaining it, however, little by little, after many a struggle, not without the loss of principles once held dear. Nor was there in the early days any system of doctrine. This does not, of course, mean that there was no belief. When Christians met to worship God, it is needless to say that they implicitly professed belief in the divine existence and in the divine unity. But they had no articles of faith, no explicit creed, no doctrine

reduced to accurate form. When people feel themselves brethren in virtue of a common enthusiasm, they do not pause to speculate on the precise nature of the bond which unites them. Passionate affection precludes the need of theories about affection or of formal contract.

(2) Such was the case with the first disciples of Jesus, and two facts may help us to realise the contrast between the spontaneous unity of the early and the formal unity of the later church. Let us turn first to the ecclesiastical position of St. Paul. By nature and training he was pre-eminently a theologian. We are all familiar with his theories on the law, on divine election, on the 'Lord from heaven,' the pre-existent man Christ Jesus. Yet what are the conditions of church-membership with this theological apostle? He recognises one condition only and with that he is satisfied. 'No man can say Jesus 'is Lord, but in the Holy Spirit.' It is easy to see what variety of theological view, what absence of any definite theological view, might lurk under the honest and ready utterance of these words. The second fact is taken from literature external to the New Testament. Most Christian churches at the present day retain and use a confession of faith known as the Apostles' creed. It is simple enough, if we compare it with the more elaborate symbols by which it was supplemented afterwards. For the most part it is confined to a confession of the one God, and certain statements about the life, death, and resurrection of Jesus. Nothwithstanding this, every tyro in church history is aware that the creed in question is no composition of the Apostles. In its most rudimentary form it can be traced to the middle of the second century, when it arose in the midst of the strifes which were sundering

Christian from Christian, sect from sect. The developed form in which we now know it, is due to accretions which it received as late as the fifth century. The fact is instructive in several ways. The Apostles formulated no creed: had they done so, the Church would not have been driven to devise a creed of its own and then attribute it to the Apostles. The age of creeds is in important respects diametrically opposed to that of the Apostles. We see that the Church had lost touch with the Apostolic age when it fathered its own rule of faith upon the Apostles. Such an anachronism could not have been committed save in a time which was creative but not critical, which had in other words no sense of historical differences.

## § 2. Influence of Greek Converts.

(1) Yet it would be pedantic bigotry to quarrel with historical Christianity because it could not escape the laws of growth and change. Great ideas are fruitful just so far as they can adapt themselves to new surroundings and unite themselves with those other ideas which represent the best moral and intellectual results of the time. The followers of Mohammed repeat with singular fidelity the lessons of their teacher, though on Persian soil Islam assimilated foreign elements and was changed into forms which Mohammed himself would have rejected with horror. But the reason why a large proportion of Moslems stand much where their prophet left them, is that on the one hand their prophet had little or nothing to say which was really new, that he taught an abstract

## CHANGES IN THE SECOND CENTURY

monotheism which is exceedingly dry and barren, and on the other hand that Moslem nations, despite their intellectual acquisitiveness, have shewn little originality and have long since been stricken with intellectual barrenness. With the religion of Jesus it was far otherwise. His teaching was simple—but it opened out endless vistas both for thought and practice. When he taught men to trust God as their Father, his words may be described as simple; yet who can ever exhaust their meaning or state the limits of their application to the progress of mankind?

(2) Again, the religion of Jesus fell on good soil. It soon passed beyond the boundaries of the Jewish population, and after a time educated heathen entered the Christian communities.

(a) It needs no great imagination to form some notion of the questions which such a person would have to ask himself. Let us suppose that he had studied Greek philosophy and literature. He would be struck by points of similarity and even identity between the lessons he had previously learned and the teaching of Jesus. How was this kinship of thought to be explained? Had Jesus borrowed from the Greeks? Or they from Jesus? Or both from a common source? Philosophy, too, had much to say on matters about which Christ and the first disciples said little or nothing. Philosophers had their views about the origin of the world, the relations of matter and spirit, the constituent elements of human nature. Did Christianity throw any light on the disputes concerning these matters which agitated the philosophic schools? Could the new truth given by Jesus be stated and defended in philosophic language?

H

(*b*) Above all, an educated convert such as we have been describing, could not help making an enormous change in Christianity, because, however reverent and humble he might be, he would be sure to seek theory and system. That was a want of the Greek mind, and of every mind moulded by Greek education. In the Old Testament generally, and in the first three Gospels which are the comparatively authentic records of Christ's teaching, there is very little formal reasoning. St. Paul does reason constantly and acutely: yet even he reasons very little, at least consciously and in set form, from the nature of things. Generally speaking, he borrows his premises from an authoritative document, viz.: the Old Testament. A philosophic heathen would require something more and something different from anything given by Jesus or Paul. And he would feel the same need with additional force, if he had to recommend his new faith to the educated world around him. Translated into the terms of Greek thought, Christianity underwent an inner change. Words and thoughts are indissolubly connected, so that a man's style is himself and a change in words that are worth anything means a change in ideas.

(3) Besides, by the process mentioned, Christianity was made to answer questions which had probably never occurred to Jesus and the first generation of his disciples, questions to which assuredly they had left no answer. The answers devised by Christian philosophers might be true, they might even be such as Jesus would have given, had the same problems presented themselves clearly to his mind. This does not alter the fact that the Christian point of view was changed, that a religion of trust and hope was tending to become a speculative

system. Great as this change was, it led the way to one much greater. Christian speculation began without pretending to be more than individual opinion. Gradually, however, these speculations, or rather a selection from them, were reduced to more complete order and consistency, till at last they won their place as part of the church's faith. Orthodoxy or right opinion became the test of a man's claim to Christian communion and the privileges which it entailed. That was nothing less than a revolution in the history of Christianity, if the name of revolution may be given to a change which was effected by almost imperceptible degrees. Here, however, we are straying beyond the limits of the present chapter.

### § 3. Philosophic Treatment of Judaism.

The writers who first undertook the task of clothing the Christian religion in philosophic garb had a precedent ready to hand. The same mode of treatment had been applied to Judaism by Jewish authors, of whom Philo is the most famous, and the only one whose works have survived.

(1) Philo was an Alexandrian Jew of priestly family. His brother held a high position in the management of the Egyptian finance, and was well known at the Imperial court. Philo himself went on an embassy to Rome, to plead the cause of the Alexandrian Jews who were then suffering persecution. This was in the year 39 A.D., and since Philo was already an old man, he must have been born some time before Jesus. It was only exceptional

circumstances which drew him from the studies to which his life was devoted. These studies were strangely unlike those of the later Rabbis, or of Jews who were his contemporaries in Palestine, the land of his fathers. Greek was his mother-tongue, and it is the Greek version of the Old Testament, not the original Hebrew text, on which Philo comments, and which he makes the basis of his reasoning. To a great extent his ideas as well as his speech were Greek. Not that he was faithless to the Jewish law. Far from that, he had the most slavish belief in its inspiration, he believed in the special providence which had chosen and ever watched over Israel, he had no doubt as to the utter superiority of Jewish religion over heathenism. Nevertheless, he was deeply and widely read in Greek literature. If the Greek philosophy had the strongest attraction for him, he also made free use of the Greek poets, and in philosophy his taste was extremely catholic. Plato and the Stoics have left the deepest impress on his writings, but he was also influenced by the Pythagoreans and by Aristotle; nor did any form of Greek speculation come amiss to him except the irreligious theory of the Epicureans. It would be much less than the truth to say that he speaks of Greek philosophers with respect. He speaks of Plato as the holy and the great, of Heraclitus as great and celebrated in many a song, of Parmenides, Empedocles, Zeno, and Cleanthes as divine men, who form a holy company.[1] In metaphysics Philo was a mere learner: he repeated for the most part what the Greeks had said before. But he had a fine aptitude for psychological enquiry, and in

[1] *Quis. rer. div. haer.* 43; *De Provid.* II. 42, 48.

this department he made valuable and original contributions.

No man could spend a long life in studies such as these without drifting far from the theology of a Scribe at Jerusalem who devoted himself to the letter of the Pentateuch. Like a true Jew, Philo laid the greatest stress on the unity of God, and abhorred idolatry. But he also held views foreign to true Judaism and indeed opposed to it. And even if no account had to be taken of the foreign matter which Philo united with the religion of the Old Testament, a real change would have been made by the very fact that he strove to reduce its manifold teaching to order and rational system.

(2) Like the Stoics, and unlike the Hebrew writers, Philo attached great value to cosmology, *i.e.*, to a theory on the origin and constitution of the world.

(*a*) It is true that the Hebrew Bible, as it existed in Philo's time and still exists in ours, opens with two accounts of the way in which the world and mankind were created. But in the rest of the Hebrew Bible, nothing is made of these accounts, no inference is drawn from them, no theory is built upon them; and the fact that the two stories are inconsistent in spirit and in detail is in itself signal proof that the Hebrews, both before the exile and for long after it, gave themselves little trouble about philosophical questions. Philo, on the contrary, felt himself impelled to the study of cosmology. His desire was to live in accordance with nature. This was the lesson he had learned from the Stoics. Therefore he must know what nature really was.

(*b*) He derived from Plato the conception of the opposition between the intellectual and the material world. The two stand over against each other. God is the absolute mind or spirit, and from all eternity the ideal patterns of created things have been present to Him. These ideal patterns cannot be perfectly copied in material objects, for matter is the region of disorder and imperfection, and cannot therefore perfectly reflect the divine idea. God is raised high above all contact with matter. No eye can see Him, no bodily ear catch the sound of His voice : nay, He is above the reach of all created intelligence : it is in ecstacy and mystical contemplation that the spirit of man approaches Him most nearly. Yet, although God be far off in one sense, in another He is very near. He is not only transcendent, *i.e.*, beyond the world : He is also immanent, *i.e.*, within it. He is remote in His essence : He is omnipresent by His ceaseless energy. He does not create matter, which, as destitute of real being, cannot come from Him who is the one true being: but He moulds matter and reduces it to all the order of which it is capable. His goodness brought our world into being : His power orders it. All things are the imperfect likeness of the *logoi*, the reasons, the ideas, the patterns, which pre-exist in the divine mind. Again these *logoi* (the term is borrowed from the Stoics) are also creative forces, immanent in things. Sometimes they are described as personal beings and identified with the angels of the Hebrew Bible. Sometimes for the many *logoi* or reasons we have the one *Logos*, the reason, the creative energy of God. This Logos is one with that divine Wisdom which is prominent in the first portion of the book of Proverbs, and which is there described by poetical license, as a personal being. To the Stoics, the Logos was simply the soul of the world, the divine element present in it. But Philo held fast to the Platonic theory that God transcends the world. Hence to him, the Logos is a secondary God. He is not the absolute God, but the connecting link between God and the world. He is the reflection of the divine essence, the idea after which all things have been framed, in whom, as the eternal high-priest, God and the world are for ever reconciled.

(*c*) After all, the reconciliation is imperfect, for matter cannot be entirely subdued by spirit. Man imprisoned in his present material body does not correspond to the ideal man, as he pre-existed in the divine mind. The senses are the well-spring of desire and of sin. The wise man must withdraw himself from the world, and follow a life of contemplation. He is to die to the body, that he may partake in the incorruptible life of God.

(3) In such teaching it is easy to find on the one hand the method and the premises of the Catholic theologian, on the other, those ascetical ideas which had their logical issue in the life of the Catholic monk. But we may be puzzled to undertand how Philo devised a system which at once, in its merits and defects, stands in sharp contrast to the teaching of the Hebrew Bible, and yet remained a sincere and loyal Jew. The answer is that Philo adopted, and could not well help adopting, that allegorical method of interpretation which had long been fashionable in the philosophic schools. He dealt with the Old Testament just as the Stoics dealt with the stories in Homer. The Bible, he thought, must contain an answer to every philosophic question, for with a simplicity wonderful to us, but quite congenial to the uncritical age in which he lived, he assumed that the questions which engrossed his

attention also occupied that of the sacred writers. Further, he took for granted that the rudest and simplest narrative was meant to convey some mysterious sense. Hence, instead of being shocked at the gross anthropomorphisms and the frequent contradictions which occur in the Bible, Philo welcomed them. They were designed to startle, and so to arouse reflection. Their object was to compel the conviction that the literal sense could not be intended, and that therefore a hidden meaning must be sought beneath the surface. Accordingly, Philo seeks and finds that hidden meaning, not here and there, or now and then, but everywhere and always. This he did on set system, after rules which, fantastic as they are, are nevertheless elaborate. For example, in commenting on the story of creation, as told in Genesis, Philo extracts a moral and metaphysical meaning from the minutest and the most unlikely details. The creation of heaven and earth means the creation of intellect and sensuous perception. The four rivers of Paradise indicate the four cardinal virtues. When the sacred writer says, ' The ' gold of that land is good,' he wishes us to understand that ' there is a twofold kind of intelligence, that which is ' concerned with the universal, and that which is concerned ' with the particular. Particular intelligence in me is not ' good, for it perishes with my death. But the divine ' intelligence dealing with the universal, that intelligence ' which dwells in the wisdom of God and in His house, ' is good, for it dwells itself imperishable in an imperish- ' able house.' And so on *ad infinitum*.

§ 4. The Apologists as Christian Philosophers.

In Philo, we see the effect which the Roman Empire produced on Jewish religion and morality. Both were changed, not only in form, but also in substance. In Judaism, however, the effect was transient. The Jewish teachers soon returned to the old groove, and Philo had no successors. Philo's real place is not in the synagogue, but in the Christian, or, as we should perhaps rather say, in the Catholic Church. Philo did what he could to fit Judaism to become the religion of the world. He tried and he failed. But the task as it fell from his hands was taken up by Christian teachers.

(1) Even in portions of the New Testament the influence of Greek philosophy is distinctly visible. But with one or two exceptions the influence of Greek ideas, of Hellenism, as it has been called, is not the result of deliberate choice on the part of the New Testament writers. The authors known as Apostolic Fathers keep to the same lines. Their Christianity consists in personal devotion to their master Christ, in the sense of a new life inspired by fresh trust and hope, in the feeling of brotherhood to men, and especially to their fellow-Christians. This happy and natural state of things could not last. Reflection must supervene, when educated men entered the Christian fold, and had to justify their conversion before the heathen world. The need of this justification was all the stronger, because Christianity, once known and seen to be distinct from Judaism, suffered persecution. But how was it to be justified? Even the simpler and earlier Christians had a controversial reasoning of their own. Only their

weapons were insufficient in the new kind of warfare. We may take the arguments said in the Acts of the Apostles to have been used by Stephen, or Peter and Paul, as samples of early controversy. With one notable exception, St. Paul's speech before the Areopagus, they turn on the claims of Jesus to be the Messiah.

(2) This was suitable enough, so long as the Christian teacher had to convince Jews or Jewish proselytes. This method, however, was passing out of date in the second century. The stream of Christian thought was parting from that of the synagogue, and henceforth, they were to pursue opposite directions, which led them far asunder. The heathen whom the church was now striving to win, could not be convinced by the sole authority of Hebrew Scriptures, with which they had often no acquaintance. The new religion had to be defended against charges of immorality, of atheism, of disloyalty to the state. It had to be proved consonant with human reason, *i.e.*, with the best reason of the day. Thus it was that Philo's work was begun again, not only with some measure of Philo's spirit, but also to some extent with the ideas which he had bequeathed, and even in his very terms. The men who undertook this learned defence of, or 'apology for' Christianity are called the Apologists. Their 'Apology,' or defence, is one of the first mile-stones on that long road which Christianity was to travel in the coming ages. One single word expresses the distance to which they had already travelled from the ground occupied by their predecessors, and that word is 'philosophy.' It is a word which occurs once only in the whole range of New Testament literature, and then it does not stand in good company. 'Take heed,' says the author of the epistle to

## THE APOLOGISTS 107

the Colossians, 'lest there be anyone that maketh spoil of 'you, through his philosophy and vain deceit, after the 'tradition of men, after the elements of the world, and 'not after Christ.' In like spirit St. Paul had reminded the Corinthians that 'not many wise after the flesh' were called to faith in Christ. The tone of the Apolgists is wholly different.

(3) The earliest among them, Quadratus and Aristides, are said by the father of Church History to have written apologies for Christianity, and to have presented them to Hadrian during his visit to Athens in the year 125.[1] The Apology of Quadratus has perished, but a Syriac translation of that of Aristides has recently been discovered in the library of the Convent of St. Catharine upon Mount Sinai. It compares the teachings of the Christians about God with those of the Barbarians, Greeks, and Jews, in the spirit of a professed philosopher, and justifies the statement of St. Jerome, that it 'was woven out of the maxims of philosophers.'[2] Aristides was consciously or unconsciously following Philo, who speaks of 'our hereditary philosophy,' 'the Jewish

---

[1] Euseb. *Eccl. Hist.* iv. 3, and *Chron.* at the year 125 A.D.

[2] Jerome, *Ep.* 70, Ad Magn. The title of the Syriac version expressly designates Aristides as 'the Philosopher.' See *Texts and Studies*, edited by J. Armitage Robinson, M.A., vol. i., No. 1; Cambridge, 1891. Prof. Rendel Harris, the discoverer of the Syriac copy, believes that Eusebius was mistaken in his date, and that the work belongs to the earlier years of Hadrian's successsor, Antoninus Pius. But compare the remarks of Mr. Robinson, p. 75, who cleverly detected a large portion of the original Greek embedded in an early mediæval romance entitled 'the Life of 'Barlaam and Josaphat.'

philosophy,' 'the philosophy according to Moses.'[1] A little later, Justin, after he had become a Christian, still professed himself a philosopher, and extolled the religion of his choice as the 'only safe and helpful philosophy.'[2] Melito, bishop of Sardis, pleading the cause of the Christian religion before M. Aurelius spoke of it, as 'our philosophy.'[3] Thenceforth, among a large section of Christians, philosophy, which represented the greatest intellectual efforts of the Greeks, became an accepted name for Christianity rightly understood. In the end, philosophic theories were made part and parcel of the Christian creed. For many at this day, to whom Plato is a mere name, Platonic speculation lives in the dogmas which they have learnt from their catechism, and their conceptions of life and duty are coloured by the ideas and terminology of the Stoics.

## § 5. The Chief Apologists.

Before entering on the doctrine of the Apologists, it will be well to say a little by way of preface on their names and lives. Of those whose writings have perished or only survive in fragments quoted by other writers, the briefest notice must suffice. Quadratus and Aristides, both resident at Athens, wrote, as we have seen, one under Hadrian, the other (perhaps) under his successor. Melito, a notable figure in the Church of Asia Minor,

[1] *Leg. ad Cai.* 23, 33, *de Mut. Nom.* 39.
[2] *Dialogue with Trypho*, 8.
[3] Quoted by Eusebius, *Eccl. Hist.* iv. 26, 27

and a fruitful writer, Claudius Apollinaris, of Hierapolis, and Miltiades, an Athenian rhetorician, addressed their apologies to M. Aurelius. The little treatise of Aristides, in spite of many features of interest to the student, would give us an extremely meagre view of the nature and grounds of Christian truth. Fortunately, we still possess three writings of Justin Martyr, who more than any other Apologist, forwarded the transformation of Christianity under Greek influences, and laid the foundations of Catholic theology.

(1) He was born about the year 100, in Flavia Neapolis, the ancient Shechem, the modern Nablus. The city had of course been Samaritan, but Justin's family probably belonged to the number of the Roman colonists settled there, and it is certain that he was brought up in paganism. He has left us an account of his early studies and of his conversion,[1] which, whether it be meant for literal fact or not, is at all events interesting, because it conveys an idea of the way in which the educated heathen of Justin's time might be and possibly were drawn to Christianity. If a romance, it is a romance describing contemporary manners. Justin then, according to his own account, came to know different exponents of the chief philosophical systems. First he betook himself to a Stoic, but, after studying under him for a considerable time, found that the Stoic had no information to give about God, and did not even consider such knowledge essential. An Aristotelian to whom he went next, repelled him by clamouring for a fee. A Pythagorean, who was his third instructor, dismissed him because he lacked previous training in music, geometry, and astronomy.

[1] *Dialogue with Trypho*, 2-8.

At last, a Platonist, a wise and worthy man, came to the town, and with him for a time, Justin seemed to fare much better. Every day added to his progress: his mind rose on the wings of contemplation, and he actually hoped that he would soon have that vision of God on which the Platonists discoursed. From these dreams he was awakened by an old man, who led him to the study of the Hebrew Scriptures, and impressed upon him the need of a revelation. He became a Christian, but continued to be a philosopher, and wandering from place to place, like the Sophists of that time, he laboured for the diffusion of the Christian faith. Of his works we still have two apologies written under Marcus Aurelius (between 147 and 160), besides a dialogue with the Jew Trypho, written somewhat later than the apologies. He died a martyr's death at Rome, about 165.

(2) Justin's pupil, Tatian, has left us an 'Address to 'the Greeks,' and here we may remark once for all that the word Greek as used by writers of this period, connotes rather what we should call educated heathen, than any special nationality. Tatian was born in Assyria, but, whatever his origin may have been, shared in the training and ideas of the Græco-Roman world. In time, Tatian struck out a path for himself different from that of his master. He became a rigid ascetic, and attached himself to a sect which condemned marriage and the use of flesh-meat and wine as intrinsically evil.

Of Athenagoras, who is supposed to have been an Athenian, we know scarcely anything, except that his 'Supplication for the Christians' was directed to Marcus Aurelius about the year 177. He was in the main a Platonist.

All the writers named wrote in Greek, although Justin and Tatian lived and laboured at Rome. Minucius Felix, on the contrary, wrote in elegant Latin. If recent scholars are correct in placing him under Marcus Aurelius, he is the earliest known author who contributed to Christian literature in that language.

The list of the Apologists just given has not the least pretension to completeness. It is only meant to afford the reader who is still strange to the subject, that preliminary knowledge which must precede any intelligent attempt to appreciate the position and teaching of the Apologists. We have now to consider that teaching, to enquire how the Apologists defended Christianity, and what the Christianity which they undertook to defend really was. For we shall find that their work was not only conservative but creative. The Christianity of which they were the champions, changed much of its character in their hands.

§ 6. Their Attitude to Judaism.

The Apologists in general boldly advance the claims of the Christian religion to rank as a philosophy. True, we should give the name of religion to much which with them passes for philosophy. So far, however, they only followed the bent of the time in which they lived, for all philosophy tended to merge in religion. But just as the philosophical religion of Marcus Aurelius differed widely from the mythology of Paganism, so the religion of the Apologists was separated by a great gulf from Judaism with its local worship and its ceremonial observances.

(1) St. Paul contended for the kernel of religion against these husks in which it had been enwrapped. The Apologists did not so much contend against them as ignore them. They had no need to struggle against the yoke of Jewish observance. They had never felt its weight, for they had been born and bred in heathenism. They had no great need even to argue with judaising Christians, because in the second century the church drew her converts almost entirely from the pagan world, and it was only 'some few persons' from the Jews and Samaritans who believed in Christ.[1] For a similar reason the Apologists were able to draw a distinction unknown to St. Paul. He looked upon the law as one, and from an historical point of view he was completely justified. The Pentateuch puts abstinence from forbidden food on the same level as the avoidance of the most appalling immorality. To St. Paul, as a true Jew, the law was one and indivisible. He who was bound by a single precept was bound by all: the modern distinction between moral and ceremonial precepts would have been unintelligible to him. The Apologists by a natural instinct assimilated the moral teaching of the Hebrew Bible, its monotheism, its conception of a divine kingdom, a people or church of God, while, justifying the distinction by various theories which there is no occasion to mention in this place, they rejected the ritual and merely national elements. Thus they were the advocates of monotheism, of belief in God's spiritual nature, and in the immortality of the soul, of a pure morality, higher than that in vogue around them, incomparably higher than that which could be gathered from the popular mythology. We are now in a position

[1] Justin, *First Apology*, 53.

to understand why they claimed for Christianity the title of philosophy, why Justin, for example, loves to speak of Christ as 'the teacher.'

(2) In fact, their philosophical religion presents many points of contact with that advanced about the same time or a little earlier by Plutarch. They were successful, because they supplied that rational religion which was a desideratum of their age. But harmony with the spirit and needs of the age is only one condition of success. Another, and a no less indispensable condition is that he who meets the popular demand should have some advantage over his rivals. Now the Apologists had this advantage and had it clearly. They could invoke religion in aid of philosophy as Plutarch and his fellows could not. Most men, even if educated, would not trust themselves (how few will trust themselves now!) to reason alone as the basis of religion. They were wearied and perplexed by the disputes of the philosophers. Had God never spoken directly and miraculously to his creatures, so closing the anxious controversy? The Apologists answered that God had so spoken through the Hebrew law-giver and prophets, and through Jesus His Son. He had set His seal to the best conclusions of human reason and had removed further doubt. It is true that heathen philosophers could and did appeal to Greek myths interpreted on the allegorical method. It is no less true that parts of the Hebrew Bible are anterior to Monotheism, and that frequently both its religion and morality betray a coarseness and narrowness ill suited to the purpose of the Apologists, and sure to give just offence to the best among the heathen. The Apologists could not, any more than the Stoics, do without recourse

I

to allegorical exposition. Still, all this being granted, the advantage which they had, was not seriously diminished. The Hebrew religion had received a large infusion of morality. The law, though by no means wholly, is yet largely moral. Passage after passage might be quoted from the prophets, in which they urge the righteousness of God and the folly of thinking to do him acceptable service by ritual divorced from morality. To this there was no parallel in the Roman Empire. The current religion was a worship of natural forces which are non-moral. The Jew might boast (and with important modifications his boast was justified) that the law of his God was 'pure, converting 'the heart.' It would be ridiculous to say as much of the Greek mythology. The Homeric gods were guilty of deeds which the Homeric heroes would have been ashamed of. The ethics of the Homeric mythology fell short of Homer's own morality, immeasurably short of Plutarch's.

### § 7. Justin and the Doctrine of the Logos.

We begin with the chief of the early Apologists whose writings have reached us.

(1) Justin inherited from Philo the notion of the Logos, the inner reason and the outward or spoken word of God. But he expressed much more clearly and emphatically than Philo his belief in the personality of this Word.

(*a*) At first, indeed, the Word was latent in the divine nature, as its impersonal reason, but when God intended to create, the Word was born into personal existence, and through him all things were made. We have striking proof of the distance to which Justin had travelled from the old Jewish and Christian position in the explanation which he gives of the title Christ. It belongs, he says, to the Word, because he was 'anointed and because ' God ordered all things through him.'[1] Can we imagine a more extraordinary instance of the action exercised by Greek philosophy on the Christian belief? Here is a title given first to all the Hebrew kings, who were anointed for their office, then to that ideal King whom the prophets announced and who was to reign in righteousness, lastly to Jesus because, as it was supposed, he was the fulfilment of the prophetic aspirations. Whereas in Justin's hands the name receives a purely Greek and philosophic application.

(*b*) This personal Word is not co-equal with the supreme being. But he is to be 'loved and worshipped ' after the God, who is unbegotten and ineffable.'[2] He has ever been the organ of revelation in the world which was made through him. The Stoics treated admirably of ethical science. Heraclitus knew what a good life was and led it. Why? ' By virtue of that seed of the Word ' which is congenital to every race of men.'[3] Hence, ' all ' that has been well said among all belongs to us ' Christians,'[4] the disciples of the Word. Nor does Justin stop here. He maintains that ' those who have lived with ' reason, are Christians, even if they were reputed Atheists, ' such for example as Socrates and Heraclitus and others ' like-minded among the Greeks, and among barbarians,

[1] *Second Apology*, 6.   [2] *Second Apology*, 13.
[3] *Second Apology*, 8.   [4] *Second Apology*, 13.

'Abraham and Ananias and Azarias and Misael and 'Elias and many others.'[1] Nay, he puts Socrates and Jesus side by side. Idolatry, he says, was 'refuted 'not only among the Greeks by Socrates with the 'help of reason, but also among the barbarians by 'the Logos himself, who took [human] form and 'was called Christ.'[2] Never were the tables more completely turned. The hand of Marcus Aurelius fell heavily upon the Christian name on the ground that it was a new and therefore an unlawful religion. In reality, it was, if Justin was to be believed, the religion of Socrates, whose memory the philosopher upon the throne revered, of Socrates, who for its sake had endured the reproach of atheism and the penalty of death. The 'new religion' was older than Socrates: it was coeval with the world. The 'barbarian' religion had been defended by the wisest of the Greeks and sealed by the testimony of his blood.

(2) Were this the whole of Justin's teaching, we might well be at a loss to understand why he faced the trouble and danger of becoming a Christian. His position resembles on one side that of a modern like Lessing, who might have found himself at home in every religion. Only, however, on one side. Justin reckoned philosophy, as the unaided effort of the human reason, insufficient for the search after God. Its weakness and proneness to error were attested by the discord among those who professed to have discovered the truth. Moreover, men were beset by malicious demons ever eager to seduce them into a vicious idolatry, that they might secure divine worship for themselves. The universality of polytheism

[1] *First Apology*, 46.   [2] *First Apology*, 5.

## JUSTIN AND THE LOGOS

was evidence of the havoc which these demons had wrought. To remedy this defect, the Word who is the angel and minister of the supreme God, had spoken by the prophets and had appeared in bodily form to the Patriarchs. In the last days this Word had taken flesh, had lived upon the earth and instructed men, in the person of Jesus Christ. We may be tempted to regard this part of Justin's theory as a reversion to the mythological type, and a fall from the liberal and impartial position of philosophy. So it was if we judge it by our modern standard. Further, it must be granted that Justin is inconsistent. We have heard him admitting that Greek philosophers were disciples of the truth, and explaining their agreement with his own conception of the Christian religion on the purely Stoical theory that the Word had scattered everywhere the 'seeds' of the truth. In some cases these seeds had fallen on barren, in others on rocky soil, for there were false philosophers, just as there were false Christians.

(3) Side by side with this admission, we find another theory which practically amounts to a total denial of the former view. The second theory is that the wise men among the Greeks derived all the sound knowledge of religion which they had, from the Hebrews. Justin states this in the plainest and most unqualified manner. 'Moses is older than all the writers among the Greeks. 'And in all that philosophers and poets have said about 'the immortality of the soul, punishments after death, the 'contemplation of heavenly things or the like, they have 'been enabled to understand [the truth] and have set 'it forth, because they got the start from the prophets.'[1]

[1] *First Apology*, 44.

'Plato borrowed from our teachers, we mean from the 'Word which came through the prophets, when he said 'that God made the world by changing formless matter.'[1] It would be a waste of words to enlarge on the radical dissimilarity between Moses and Plato, or the naïveté of the supposition that the latter could have borrowed from the former. Justin's method is quite as unphilosophical in his elaborate argument that Christ is the very or essential Word of God, so that those who follow him as their guide are better off than Platonists or Stoics can possibly be. Justin's arguments are drawn in the main from the Greek translation of the Hebrew Scriptures, interpreted on that same arbitrary system in which Philo had led the way, and in which any text could prove anything. Christ is shewn to be the Word in human form, because long before his coming the sacred writers had by miraculous inspiration predicted the time of his advent and the minutest details of his life. A single specimen will enable the reader to form some conception of the way in which Justin goes to work. In the blessing of Jacob, Judah is portrayed as 'Binding his foal unto the vine, 'and his ass's colt unto the choice vine; he hath washed 'his garments in wine, and his vesture in the blood of 'grapes.' This very simple passage which paints in poetical colours the fertility of Judah, is adduced by Justin no less than five times. The ass's colt denotes on the one hand the literal colt which carried Christ into Jerusalem, on the other, the gentile converts whom Christ reduced to the obedience of faith. The washing in wine signifies the blood in which Christ washes his people. The blood is called the blood of the vine, to indicate that the blood of

[1] *First Apology*, 59.

Jesus was drawn from the power of God and not from human generation.[1] This brief summary spares the reader the tedium of Justin's long exposition. One would have thought that Justin might have been content with the Jewish Scriptures, if permitted to handle them in this free manner. But besides making the Hebrew Bible speak Christian language, he accuses the Jews of wilfully mutilating the text,[2] a charge which Justin, who was himself anything but a model of accuracy in quotation, brings without the least reason.

(4) We have long outgrown the exegesis of Justin, and it may seem hardly worth while to dwell upon it. But it does deserve attention, because it prevailed for many centuries in the church and is not quite dead even now. And it suited Justin's time, if it does not suit ours. Moreover, in his doctrine of the Word Justin helped to build up that Christian or Catholic theology which ultimately became the religion of the Empire. Partly this theology triumphed, because it adopted and incorporated the philosophy of the Empire. The educated heathen were ready to accept the proposition that the Logos or reason is the Son of God. Partly it triumphed, not because of that which it took from, but because of that which it gave to the Empire, namely, a moral and comparatively rational religion. Despite his oddities, as we, uncritically perhaps, can scarcely help calling them, Justin mingled philosophy and religion with no small skill, and adjusted the proportions to the palate of the Roman world. Let us return for a moment to a saying

[1] *Dial. with Tryph.* 53, 54. Comp. 63, 76. *First Apology*, 32, 54.
[2] *Dial. with Tryph.* 71, seq.

of his which we have quoted already. Idolatry, he says, 'was refuted not only among the Greeks by Socrates, but 'also among the barbarians by the Word himself who 'took form and was called Jesus Christ.' Here Socrates and Jesus are united in the interests of philosophy, separated in the interests of religion.

(5) The Apologists do not all look out on the heathen world in the same mood. Some contemplate it much as Justin did, or go beyond him in the friendliness of their overtures to non-Christian philosophy. Thus Minucius Felix undertakes to prove the truth of Christianity from the Stoic principle of knowledge, and expresses himself in these striking words, 'I have exhibited the opinion of 'nearly all the philosophers, so that anyone would think, 'either that Christians are now philosophers or that 'philosophers were then Christians.'[1] Christianity is the wisdom which nature has implanted in man:[2] let a man use his reason in the search for truth and he will find the Christian doctrine in his own soul. He translates Christian ethics into the terminology of the Stoics, and represents the Christian community as a union of philosophers all the world over, of philosophers who are conscious of natural kindred with each other. In like manner, Athenagoras extols Plato, as one who 'contemplated the 'eternal mind and God who is apprehended by reason.'[3] But, all did not hold the same language. Tatian sets Christianity in antagonism to the teaching of the philosophers, and condemns its practical results, pride, hypocrisy, sensuality.[4] Theophilus went so far as to say that the

[1] Minucius Felix, *Octavius*, 20.  [2] *Octavius*, 16.
[3] Athenagoras, *Supplication*, 23.
[4] Tatian, *Address to the Greeks*, 2, and elsewhere.

## SUPERIORITY OF THE CHRISTIAN LIFE

philosophers were 'inspired by demons.'[1] A generation later Tertullian wrote of philosophy and philosophers in the same temper.[2] Yet Tatian often calls Christianity 'our philosophy'[3] and asserts that it introduces no new doctrine, but only the truths which mankind once had and lost.[4] Theophilus is of the same mind, and Tertullian has left us a famous treatise 'on the Testimony of the Soul 'naturally Christian.'

(6) In general the Apologists who, as has been said, are the advocates not of philosophy pure and simple, but of philosophy attested by revelation, make a point of the way in which poets and philosophers contradict each other, and even sometimes contradict themselves.[5] From this inextricable confusion the religion of Christ had in their opinion delivered mankind. They made a second point from the superiority of the Christian life. 'We do 'not speak great things,' says Minucius Felix with excusable pride, 'but we live them.'[6] Thirdly, they felt that Christ had at all events made truth current coin, whereas the philosophers had failed to do so. It was the 'simple 'style, the artless form, the comprehensible account of 'creation,' which among other reasons lured Tatian from the doctrines of the Greeks to the 'Scriptures of the 'barbarians.'[7]

---

[1] Theophilus, *To Autolycus*, ii. 8.
[2] Tertullian, *Apologeticus*, 46. *On Prescription against Heretics*, 7.
[3] Tatian, *Address*, 31, and elsewhere.
[4] *Address*, 29.
[5] See *e.g.* Theophilus, *To Autolycus*, ii. 4, 5, 8, iii. 7.
[6] Minucius Felix, *Octavius*, 38.
[7] Tatian, *Address*, 29.

## § 8. Preparation for a Dogmatic System.

We may now sum up the results of the work which the Apologists did.

(1) They equipped the Christian religion for the conquest of the Roman world by changing it into a philosophy, attested by revelation. They mingled together the metaphysics of Platonism, the doctrine of the Logos, which came from the Stoics, morality partly Platonic, partly Stoic, methods of argument and interpretation learnt from Philo, with the pregnant maxims of Jesus and the religious language of the Christian congregations. They were the fathers of theology, and of the dogmatic system, which, in the eyes of many even now, belongs to the essence of Christianity. Yet the word 'dogma' is not Christian but pagan in its origin, and as with the name, so it is with the thing. 'Dogma' was the term used for the decisions or conclusions of philosophers. A Stoic, for instance, followed the 'dogmas' of Zeno and his successors. The New Testament knows nothing of Christian dogma: when the Apostolic Fathers use the word, they do not employ it in the modern sense, but mean by it a rule of life, a disposition of providence or the like.[1] But the Apologists in their place as Christian philosophers were forced to answer the question, What are the dogmas of your philosophy? We are only repeating the same thing in other words when we add that they were the fathers of Christian theology, and it is no cause of surprise to find

[1] See the references in Lightfoot on *Coloss.* ii. 14, and on Ignatius, *To the Magnesians*, 13.

Justin speaking of 'theological enquiry' in its modern and technical sense.[1]

(2) The dogmas of Christianity then, as maintained by them, were chiefly these three, the unity of God the creator, the necessity of serving God by a holy life, the coming of the day of judgment with its rewards for the virtuous, and penalties for the vicious. Had they nothing to say about the forgiveness of sins and the redemption of the world by Christ? Justin, indeed, is fond of dilating on such topics, nor would any of the Apologists have denied their importance. But most of them give these subjects a very secondary place, and in fact, when Christianity was regarded from that philosophical point of view which the Apologists took, redemption could not any longer be the central theme. For what man wanted, was, in the eyes of the Apologists, not redemption, but revelation. He required to know the truth about God and about himself. That being given, the rest was in his own power, for the Apologists, like the later Stoics, argued strenuously that man's will was free, that if his outward circumstances were bound fast in fate, he was still master of his thoughts and actions. Thus the 'dogmas' of the Apologists were an accommodation to philosophy. Philosophy and religion up to a certain point were merged in each other. Celsus, the heathen opponent of Christianity, was ready to accept the doctrine that the Logos was the Son of God.[2] Even the idea of inspiration was admitted on both sides. It is not a Christian Apologist, it is Cicero, who wrote, 'Nobody ever became a great man without some 'divine afflatus.' And before we quit this part of the

[1] *Dialogue with Trypho*, 113.   [2] Origen, *Against Celsus*, ii. 31.

subject, let the reader notice the strange and instructive history of the word dogma. To us it expresses the antagonism, or at least the divergence, between philosophy and religion. But originally the name and the thing were borrowed from philosophy. To us dogma means something which admits of no direct proof from reason. In the hands of the Apologists, Christianity became philosophic and dogmatical at one and the same time, and each dogma was a conclusion of the human reason. A dogmatic faith is a philosophical creed. The real objection to it is, not that it ignores reason and philosophy, but that it stereotypes the philosophy of the Roman world, aud confuses Greek and Roman speculation with the religious intuitions of Jesus. Many a man has been accused of intellectual pride, just because he prefers the simplicity which is after Christ, to intellectual theories of which Jesus was wholly ignorant.

(3) As yet, however, there were but the faint beginnings of that dogmatic system which is embodied in the Catholic creeds.

(*a*) The conception of dogma, as given by the Apologists, was on the whole to remain, not, however, without serious modification. This arose from a restriction made in the function of philosophy. With the Apologists, philosophy and religion covered the same ground, and were indeed convertible terms. No doubt they drew largely from the Hebrew Scriptures and the traditions of Christ's life. But these were vital to them, not so much because they formed the actual contents of religion, as because they confirmed it by solid proof. The essence of their religion lay in beliefs, which have a certain resemblance to the deism of the last century. But the fulfilment of prophecy in Christ raised these beliefs from probability to certainty. This is why Justin puts a stress on the details of Christ's life which seems to us childish. The smallest incident, if miraculously predicted, proved Christ to be the very Logos or reason of God, and therefore the one safe teacher of a heavenly philosophy. In after ages, a distinction was made between natural religion, which embraced the deism of the Apologists, and dogmas such as those of the Trinity and Incarnation. These last were expressed in philosophical language, they were due to the action of philosophy upon the data supplied, as was thought, by the original teaching of Christ and his Apostles, but it was not pretended that they could be proved by mere reason. In the last resort, they were inferences from two premises, of which one at least was revealed. Human reason certainly could not prove dogma, and might be unable to comprehend it. Thus a far more complicated system replaced the simple philosophy of the Apologists. Men were asked to 'believe' 'in order that they might understand,' and philosophy, no longer the sister, became the hand-maid of faith.

(*b*) Again, the dogmas of the Apologists, unlike the dogmas which were advanced a century later, made no claim to rank as articles of faith. The Apologists had their own theories about the Word of God. But they were mere theories. The Catholic church was just springing into life, and so far as it existed (in Justin's time it did not exist) it imposed no theory about the Word as a condition of communion.

(*c*) Lastly, the Apologists, so far as they were the fathers of dogma, died while dogmas which began with them and afterwards attained gigantic stature, were still in their feeble infancy. They had a theology of the Word, but not of the Trinity, though the word Trinity is used for the first time by Theophilus of Antioch.[1] Their theology, moreover, differed on a point of capital importance from that of later ages. The Catholic church finally acquiesced in the belief that the Word is distinct from, but co-equal with, the Father. Instead of this, the Apologists were impelled to believe in the distinct personality of the Word, just because he was not God co-equal with the Father, but a secondary God subordinate to Him, and for that reason capable at once of manifesting the supreme Being, and coming into immediate contact with the world, as the invisible Creator of all could not do. In the Spirit as a distinct being they had little interest, and Theophilus, though he uses the word Trinity, is much at a loss to distinguish the second Person of his Trinity from the third.[2] A few words from Justin exhibit the fluid condition of a theology not yet cast into the moulds of later dogma. ' We worship and adore Him [*viz.* : God], and the Son ' who came from Him and taught us these lessons, and ' the host of the other good angels who attend on him and ' are like him, and the prophetic spirit.'[3] Here the Son is placed by implication among the angels, whose leader he is; the name of the ' prophetic spirit ' is mentioned after that of the angels. It is true that this passage may be said to represent the low-water mark in the theology of the Apologists. Not one of them, however, had even dreamt that there was a Trinity of equal Persons in the Godhead.

[1] *To Autolycus*, ii. 15.
[2] See *To Autolycus*, ii. 10, with Otto's notes.
[3] *First Apology*, 6.

# CHAPTER V.

## CHANGED ASPECTS OF CHRISTIANITY.

### § 1. Twofold Unity of Creed and Organisation.

THE works of the Apologists exhibit the rise of that theology which afterwards hardened into dogma and thoroughly altered the conception and character of Christianity. This was the most momentous change effected by the place of the Christian church in the midst of the Roman civilisation.

As yet, however, we have only seen the first signs of the transformation which was at hand. The Apologists had a theology, and one which, in its main lines, finally prevailed; but they had no dogma in the modern sense of the word, because they did not impose their speculations as articles of church communion. It was after their time, in the course of the third century, that the change set in, by which the bond of union between Christian and Christian came to consist in the acceptance of a theological creed. During that period, an intellectual was substituted for a religious and moral bond. The Christian brotherhood, once knit together by common hopes and aspirations, by the same childlike trust in God and Christ, by holiness of life and charity towards each other, tended more and more to become a body of men who held the same philosophical ideas on the nature of the Godhead. This fundamental alteration was accompanied by many others, some of which were scarcely less important. The congregations had in the early days no officials, and did not need them. They were under the influence of the spirit, or, to put it in modern language, of an enthusiasm which overpowered them. Their teachers were men who spoke as the spirit 'gave them utterance:' new churches were founded by wandering evangelists, who had been called supernaturally to this special work. The churches were one, because they were of one mind, and because they helped each other. Little by little, officials appointed by their fellow-Christians replaced the inspired teachers, and the church throughout the Empire was governed by a federation of bishops. Unity of organisation was combined with unity of creed, each unity being external and formal, whereas the old unity was internal and spontaneous. It would require a complete history of the church during the first three centuries of its existence to trace these changes in detail. But all of them are closely connected with the relations between Christianity and the Empire. For this reason, the chief among them will be briefly noted and described in this chapter, fuller information being reserved for the subsequent manuals of this series.

## § 2. Altered Relations to Judaism.

First, the Christian church cut its old moorings and lost touch with Judaism from the very fact that it was launched into the larger world and the wider interests of the Empire.

(1) Not that the severance was, or is even now, complete. The Christians carried with them valuable possessions, which had originally belonged to Palestine. Like the Jews, they continued to believe in one God : they retained, though not altogether unimpaired, the monotheism, which was the distinctive glory of later Judaism. Heathen philosophers had been in a sense monotheists. Only, however, in a sense. So far as the Christian ideas of the divine unity were clear and free from the taint of compromise with idolatry, they were not heathen, but Jewish. Nor is it too much to say that the Christian God was to a great extent identified with the God of Israel. The God of philosophy stood apart from the popular religion and easily became a mere abstraction. The Christian God, on the contrary, was a being who had spoken by the prophets, who had guided the destinies of the chosen nation, and educated it, that in the end He might bring the world to a knowledge of Himself. This at least was the view maintained, not indeed, without keen opposition, but still maintained among the vast majority of Christians. Its obvious disadvantages were counterbalanced by far greater gain. Religion was instinct with life, because it was directed to a God, who, from the first had ruled the world for righteous ends. So again, the conception of God as the creator was Jewish. The

K

philosophers of the Empire either identified God with the universe, or represented Him as moulding it from pre-existent matter: they did not reach the thought of creation out of nothing. The Hebrew Scriptures in which these ideas are enunciated with varying degrees of purity, became the authoritative Scriptures, and were till the latter part of the second century the only authoritative Scriptures, of the Christian church. The name too, and the idea of the church itself were Jewish. As national independence passed away from the Jewish people and its restoration became more and more hopeless, pious souls comforted themselves with the reflection that Israel was a religious community, 'the congregation,' or 'assembly of the Lord.' This idea assumed a nobler form in that Kingdom of God which Jesus preached. It was continued among Christians. But just as they explained the Hebrew Bible on the allegorical method in vogue at the time, and found it witnessing everywhere that Jesus was the Messiah, so to them the congregation or *ecclesia* of the Lord meant no longer the Jewish nation, or the best part of it, but rather those who, whatever their nation might be, believed in Jesus as Christ and Lord.

(2) Such were the permanent contributions of Judaism to Christian thought. For the rest, Judaism fell almost out of sight. No other result was possible, when the church was almost entirely composed of Gentile converts and their descendants.

(*a*) The controversy about the law which so vehemently agitated the minds of men in the Apostolic age settled itself by the irresistible force of circumstances. Outwardly Jesus had lived and died a Jew. No doubt the principles of his spiritual religion once accepted must be fatal to

Jewish legalism and ceremonialism. The Jewish law crumbled to pieces for those who were persuaded that 'not that which entereth into the mouth defileth a man,' that 'the Sabbath was made for man, not man for the Sabbath,' that the Mosaic law of divorce was a concession to the hardness of the heart, and contradicted the divine institution of marriage. But Jesus had no occasion to develop his principles to their utmost consequence. It was still open for Jewish disciples, so long as they were in a majority, to maintain the binding force of the Jewish law, either for believers of Jewish birth or for all, whether Jew or Gentile, who would enter that 'kingdom of God' which Jesus founded. We all know that the attempt was made. When, however, the Jewish Christians became an insignificant minority, any such attempt would have been desperate. The very claims made for Jesus to be the Messiah, as the first Christians understood the term, awoke less and less interest among the mass of Christians. The local ordinances of Judaism had no possible attraction for them. The destruction of the temple put it beyond their power to observe most important parts of the Jewish law. Of that which was left, much was impractical or even unintelligible without Jewish tradition, which had become inaccessible to most Christians.

(*b*) But there were parts of the Jewish law which did supply a desideratum among Christians. It gave revealed rules of morality not to be found so clearly and compactly stated, in the literature of Greece and Rome. Hence a distinction was made between the ceremonial and moral parts of the law. Some thought that the ceremonial precepts had been given by God, but only for the time which preceded the death of Jesus, others that they had always been intended to be taken in a purely figurative sense. It came to be generally allowed that in any case they were not binding now. This distinction has, of course, no shadow of justification in the text of the Hebrew law. It could only be made by persons who had a very superficial acquaintance with it. The prohibition of eating unclean meat for example is enforced in Leviticus for no temporary reason, but on the ground that the Israelites are to be holy as their God is holy. Nevertheless, on the part of Gentile Christians the distinction, arbitrary as it is, was inevitable. Even now it is accepted by multitudes without the slightest misgiving.

(3) This was a point of view wholly different from that of St. Paul, and in the new order of things, St. Paul's position, his theology and his arguments dropped out of sight almost as completely as that of the judaizing Christians with whom he fought. St. Paul advocated a Christianity which made salvation independent of race or of Jewish observances, and so far the church of later ages was at one with him. But here the agreement was at an end. Theologian as he was, St. Paul did not found the theology of the church. If St. Paul is in principle anti-Jewish, he is in his method of argument the most intensely Jewish among all the writers of the New Testament. He betrays at every turn a rabbinical training, which made him often unintelligible to the church which arose after he was gone. St. Paul knew the law too well to dream of separation between its moral and ceremonial elements. To him the law was one and indivisible. In his youth he had struggled to fulfil it to the least jot and tittle. He groaned under its burden and under the consciousness of sin which it evoked. At last the extremity of the evil worked its

own cure. Through 'the law he died to the law' and rose to a new life of faith or trust, and, being free from all law, passed under the dominion of love in which the law is fulfilled. His religion was in its kernel sublimely reasonable. It is not law but trust which expresses the true and personal relations between the soul and God. Yet this stand-point transcended the common-sense of average men. They want rules of conduct, tangible and definite, by which they may test themselves and others. Besides, Greeks had groaned under no burden of legal ordinances, and the experience of the great Apostle was quite strange to them. St. Paul sighed for deliverance from the law, which was 'the power of sin.' The Greek looked for deliverance from a sensual and self-indulgent life, in which the nature of sin was scarcely felt. Hence an author who writes in the name of Paul but who really lived long after his time and breathed a different air, describes Jesus as 'one who gave himself for us that he 'might redeem us from all lawlessness, and purify unto 'himself a people for his own possession zealous of good 'works.'

§ 3. New Prominence of Morality.

In the church which was free from the associations of Judaism on the one hand, and had lost the ability to understand St. Paul upon the other, morality assumed a prominence unknown either to St. Paul or to the first disciples. This statement can hardly fail to seem paradoxical and certainly it needs explanation.

(1) It may be said that the Sermon on the Mount makes morality all in all, and that the difference between Jesus and the church which was set up in his name lay in this very thing, that, whereas Jesus made goodness the one thing needful, the Catholic church imposed articles of belief and laid the chief stress upon them. This objection is plausible and it contains a certain amount of truth. It is indeed unanswerable, so long as we contrast dogma, or intellectual assent to a series of intellectual propositions, with morality. That, however, is not the real point. The contrast should be made not between morality and dogma but between morality and religion. Religion if it has any value implies morality: the amount and quality of the morality which it implies is the test of its worth. But religion is not a code of ethical rules: it is the communion of person with person, of the soul with God. Now Jesus was not a moralist but a religious teacher. Let anyone read attentively the 'Manual' of Epictetus and then turn to the 'Sermon on the Mount.' He will feel instinctively that he has passed into a different sphere. Epictetus has something to say about religion, Jesus has a great deal to say about morality. But with Epictetus the main thing is self-improvement and religion is secondary. Jesus directs the eyes of his hearers to a God who is their Father. It is from the desire to be like Him, from gratitude and love to Him that all our conception of duty is to flow. We are to show kindness to the wicked and the unthankful, because we are the children of Him who makes his sun shine on the just and the unjust: we are to forgive without stint or limit, as He has forgiven us. This is very different from the Greek notion of 'virtue,' a word which never occurs in

the gospels and is scarcely found in the whole course of the New Testament. Again Jesus gives no code of rules, though he sets forth principles few in number but capable of infinite application. What code of rules could determine the conduct of those who were to be perfect, as their Father in heaven is perfect? It is only the coarser relations of life which can be fixed by rule: friendship and love are dead, or dying, when the need of rule begins to be felt. For the same reason the disciple of Jesus can never be content with himself. When he has done all, he is 'an unprofitable servant.' He has to pray daily for forgiveness. His aim is different from that of a disciple of Epictetus, who strives to live 'according to nature,' and may hope for a fair measure of success.

(2) Very soon the Christians of the Empire felt that they could not breathe at this height. They came to think of morality and religion as two separate quantities both of which were necessary for the Christian, though of course religion was to promote morality. In the first place the Christian had to believe in God and Christ, in the second place he had to fulfil his moral obligations, and if he satisfied both requirements he would be saved. The change is marked by a significant term. Christianity was described as 'the new law.' The expression first occurs in the early epistle falsely ascribed to Barnabas,[1] was soon adopted universally, and is still retained in Roman Catholic theology. Those who introduced it, were far from being judaisers. It was not the old law with its burdensome ceremonial which they advocated, but 'the ' new law' which consisted of moral precepts. In some measure these moral precepts were derived from Jesus,

[1] *Epistle of Barnabas*, 2.

but on the whole the morality which obtained a footing in the church was simply the best morality of the Greek philosophers. In such an author as Clement of Alexandria, the language and the moral rules are to a great extent the reflection of Stoic teaching, and his Pædagogus, a manual of the ascetic life, is in considerable portions taken verbally from Musonius. This morality of the heathen philosophers was handed down to the middle ages; it appears in the *Summa* of Thomas Aquinas: it survives in many a modern treatise of Roman Catholic piety. The change dealt a heavy blow to religion. Religion implies constant dependence on God, and so long as the need of daily help and forgiveness was recognised, there was no danger that the sense of dependence would perish by disuse. But the notion that Christianity was a new law left man to work out his salvation by himself. The Christians came to think like the Stoics that virtue was in a man's own power. True, they could not as Christians ignore the need of forgiveness. But it was the common theory that forgiveness of serious offences was bestowed once for all, when a man entered the church by baptism. After that, no further forgiveness was to be expected. He who had been delivered from heathen error and the power of the demons had no further excuse. He must prepare himself to bear 'the yoke of the Lord.' To this yoke so understood human nature proved in the end inadequate, and a remedy was found in magical means of obtaining divine pardon, a remedy which often proved worse than the disease.

(3) Nor was the morality taught by any means always rational. It was deeply tinged with the asceticism which shrank from the enjoyments and even the business of life.

It forfeited no small part of that which is the distinctive glory of Christianity, viz. that it counts nothing common or unclean, that it claims every phase of human life as its own, and infuses a divine spirit into all natural relations. From the very earliest times traces of this ascetic spirit appear in the church. Even in St. Paul's time, the Roman church counted among its members men who abstained on ascetic grounds from animal food. The same spirit had been exhibited on a large scale among the Palestinian Jews, by the Essenes, who led a monastic life, abstained from flesh, and deprecated marriage. It is difficult, perhaps impossible, to ascertain the origin of this ascetism. It was not due to the Old Testament or the orthodox Judaism, and Christians could not have learnt it from a master 'who came eating and drinking.' Still, it appears, as has been just said, in the very infancy of the church, and early in the second century it had reached full stature. From whatever source it first found its way into Christian life, it was in harmony with the '*askesis*,' the ascetism of bodily training recommended by the Stoic philosophers, and with the persuasion widely spread in the ancient world that matter was the root of evil.

(4) Its prominent features were rigorous abstinence and the preference of the celibate to the married state. ' If 'thou canst bear the complete yoke of the Lord,' says the 'Teaching of the Apostles,' 'thou wilt be perfect. But if 'thou canst not, do what thou canst. As to food, bear ' what thou art able.'[1] Justin boasts that he can point to Christians of every class who have lived to old age in unmarried purity.[2] There were considerable bodies of

[1] *Teaching of the Apostles*, 6.    [2] *First Apology*, 15.

Christians who entirely repudiated marriage. Such were the early sect of Encratites, or continent persons, to whom Tatian the Apologist attached himself. Tatian wrote a treatise 'on Christian perfection,' with the object of propagating his ascetical views, and he treated marriage as a kind of immorality.[1] Many of the Gnostics were forced by their doctrine that matter was evil to the same low estimate of marriage. Others who did not consciously hold the Gnostic principle on the nature of matter, were no less extreme in practice. Thus we learn that Dionysius, of Corinth, in the seventh decade of the second century, expostulated with a Cretan bishop and begged him 'not 'to lay on the brethren the heavy yoke of enforced 'chastity, but to accommodate himself to the weakness of 'the generality.'[2] Of those who tolerated marriage, some limited their approval to marriage once in life. A second union was, as they thought, no better than 'a specious adultery.'[3] The church soon recoiled from extremes on which its future as the church of the Roman world would have suffered utter shipwreck. The repudiation of marriage, and even of second marriage, was left to the heretical sects, while the large or Catholic church pursued a more moderate and practical policy. Nevertheless the Catholic church committed itself to the principle that the celibate was holier beyond all comparison than the married state, and a long succession of fathers and saints have indulged in extravagant laudations of virginity.

[1] Clement of Alexandria, *Miscellanies*, iii. 81.
[2] Eusebius, *Eccl. Hist.* iv. 23, 7.
[3] Athenagoras, *Supplication*, 33; Theophilus, *To Autolycus*, iii. 15. The still harsher view of the Montanists is given by Tertullian, *On Monogamy*, and *Exhortation to Chastity*.

(5) The ascetical view of life thus authorised has been fruitful in pernicious results. Morbid attention has been concentrated on matters which have no place in a pure and healthy mind. The persons best fitted to give a pattern of domestic life have been withdrawn from it. By recognising two states, one of which was, though permitted, intrinsically imperfect, the church made a capitulation with human weakness, and exempted the mass of Christians from the perfection to which they are called. The absolute prohibition of marriage by the smaller churches or sects, was not only more consistent, but even in a sense more Christian. Again, the holiest relations of life in which, above all, the Christian spirit should display itself, have been degraded in the eyes of mankind and barely tolerated in concession to human weakness. Lastly, to leave the special subject of ascetism and revert to the general conception of Christianity as a new law, the new Christianity lost that power of inspiring peace and joy which the Christianity of Christ and his apostles had exhibited in an eminent degree. While Christian observance flowed naturally from Christian love, it might well be said that the commandments of Christ 'were not heavy.' The sacrifices of love are not burdensome, but self-discipline is. 'I do not know,' says a Christian writer of the second century, 'if these com-'mandments can be kept by many, inasmuch as they are 'exceedingly hard.'[1] This is the prevailing tone in Catholic piety, allayed more or less after a time by the comfort which could be afforded by trust in sacraments

[1] *Shepherd of Hermas*, 'Commandments,' xii. 3. The author adds the cold assurance that they become easy to those who make up their minds to keep them.

as channels of mysterious grace. And this comfort was counterbalanced by the growing burden of the new law which came to include ceremonial as well as moral precepts. Beginning as a reaction against the legalism of the Pharisees, Christianity was in its own turn corrupted into legalism and formalism, and Luther could enter into the mind of St. Paul, because his own experience when a monk had been like that of the apostle when a Pharisee.

## § 4. Decay of the Expectation of Christ's Second Coming.

As Christianity made its power felt in the Empire and became conscious of its strength, a new vista opened out before it, and old hopes once vivid, grew pale and died away.

(1) The early Christians were ready enough to indulge in fantastic delusions, but they never dreamt that they would convert the world. On the contrary, the hopes which they did cherish were incompatible with any such expectation. They inherited the belief held by Jewish enthusiasts, that in a little, the course of the world would be abruptly ended, and the kingdoms of the heathen be replaced by the kingdom of God and the reign of the Saints. They studied diligently that literature of the Jews which is called apocalyptic, because it professed to lift the veil which hid from view the coming catastrophe and the coming glory. The 'revelations' of Daniel, of Ezra, of Enoch, of Baruch, of Moses, were favourite books among Christians, and they produced books of their own in imitation of them or gave Jewish

'revelations' a Christian complexion by interpolating the text. Of course, the Christians modified the hopes which they inherited from the Jews. Believing Jesus to be the Christ, they naturally held that he was to come again and reign over the kingdom of the saints. All believed that the end was at hand. Even St. Paul, whose spiritual tendencies saved him from dwelling on this seductive theme, still was convinced that Christ was to appear again in his own time, and that many of the generation in which he lived, would never taste death. He had little interest in marriage, and thought slavery a matter of small moment, because no external change seemed worth while, seeing that the end was so near. But most Christians went much further. They were confident that a final struggle between good and evil was at hand, in which evil would for a time prevail, that Christ would reverse the triumph of sinners by suddenly appearing in glory, that the saints would be raised from the dead and would reign with him on earth, after which the general resurrection was to follow. 'I,' says Justin, 'and all Christians 'who are thoroughly right-minded know that the 'resurrection of the flesh will take place, and that a 'thousand years will be spent in Jerusalem, rebuilt, 'adorned, enlarged, as Ezekiel and Isaiah and the other 'prophets confess.'[1] This view prevailed everywhere in Christianity till it had been permeated and transformed by Greek influences. Papias, of Hierapolis, that zealous collector of apostolic traditions, had a wonderful story to tell of the vines in the millennium. Each plant was to produce ten thousand shoots: each shoot, ten thousand branches: each branch, ten thousand twigs: each twig,

[1] *Dialogue with Trypho,* 80.

ten thousand clusters : each cluster, ten thousand grapes: each grape was to yield twenty-five firkins of wine. If a saint put forth his hand to reach a cluster, a neighbouring cluster would cry, 'Take me, for I am better.' This nonsense is gravely repeated by Irenæus, who tells us that Papias received it from St. John, who heard it from the lips of Jesus.[1]

(2) During the whole of the first three centuries, and later, this belief lingered in the east, and it had a much stronger hold in the west. But the Greek spirit was hostile, and in the end fatal to it. It had done its work. The belief in a millenium at Jerusalem often coupled with the idea that the anti-Christian power was embodied in the Roman Empire, was naturally attractive to Jews, and when adapted to Christian forms of thought, it enabled the Christian to rival the Jewish propaganda. It was very far from attractive to philosophic Greeks, who had no desire for the restoration of Jerusalem, and to whom the doctrine of the resurrection of the flesh was odious, much more the sensual delights of a Jewish millennium. Such fantastic dreams were also ill suited to a religion in which reason was displacing enthusiasm, which was making its way in the world, and could not therefore be expected to long for the destruction of the world, which from the time of Origen, at least, began to think that the world would be converted, and would protect instead of persecuting the Christian faith. It is well worth noting that the writers who best represent the amalgamation of original Christianity with Greek ideas are indifferent to or opposed to the old belief in a millenium. The Apologists, except Justin, pass it over in silence. It

[1] Irenæus, *Against Heresies*, v. 33, 3.

was vigorously attacked in the great Alexandrian school by the philosophic Origen. The new teachers were occupied with the hope of spiritual incorruption and immortality, and with the thought of mystical union with God as a present possession. Their allegorical method of interpretation enabled them to neutralise the passages in the prophets, and in the Revelation of St. John, which told for their Millenarian adversaries, though the leaders of the Alexandrian school did not conceal their aversion to the latter book, and for a time openly rejected its authority. The western Christians were less philosophical and more conservative, consequently Millenarianism held its ground there, after it had been driven from the learned churches of the east and only lingered in obscure corners of the eastern world.

# CHAPTER VI.

## THE ATTEMPT TO MAKE CHRISTIANITY AN INTELLECTUAL SYSTEM.

MEANTIME, nothing has been said of the internal difficulties which Christianity had to overcome before it could vanquish its external enemies and grow into the church of the Empire. So long as we look simply to the work of the Apologists, to the gradual and natural fusion of Christianity with ideas borrowed from the heathen world, and to the instinct by which Christians allowed reflection to replace enthusiasm, and abandoned hopes once dear to the Christian heart, but unsuitable to the changed position of the church, all seems easy and plain. But much remains to complete the account we have given.

### § 1. Dangers arising from Contact with Greek Thought.

(1) It was impossible that educated Christians should bring the new religion into contact with Greek thought and not expose it to grave peril. What security could

there be that Greek ideas might not mingle with Christianity till the distinctive features of the latter were obliterated? Christianity might have found its level among the philosophical schools of the time. In this case it might have escaped persecution and perhaps obloquy, but it would have paid dearly for this by losing its hopes of conquest. Again, reasoning and speculation tend to divide men who have been united by community of feeling. It was possible therefore that Christians might be split up into a number of sects, none of which stood out conspicuous by its numbers and influence above the rest. In that case also the Christian religion could scarcely have had any chance of success. For there was yet no great or Catholic church overshadowing the sects and bound together by an organisation of its own. There was no single body claiming authority to regulate the formation of doctrine, to discriminate between truth and error, and so to secure, at least among the large majority of Christians, unity of belief and of discipline. There was no collection of Christian books separated by common consent from the general mass of Christian literature, and recognised as the authentic sources of Christian belief. There was no Catholic church, and no New Testament. Christians reverenced the Hebrew Scriptures, but they had from the first subjected them to an allegorical interpretation by which almost any meaning might be drawn from their pages. They sedulously preserved traditions about the life and sayings of Jesus, but such tradition was necessarily fluid, and was constantly changing as it passed from mouth to mouth, from church to church, from one generation to another.

L

(2) The danger of disintegration, which might have been expected, soon became painfully evident. The Apologists availed themselves of Greek ideas, but they did so with moderation. Others, before and after them, did not restrain themselves within the same limits. The old Christianity was transformed in the boldest fashion till hardly one of its original features could be recognised. The extremity of danger called forth the appropriate remedy, which was the Catholic church. That body with its fixed organisation stemmed the flood of extravagant speculation. Its officers contrived to unite the great body of Christians. It made a selection from Christian literature and tradition, affixing to each the seal of its authority. It decided with practical tact how far Greek speculation might be safely endured. It won the day because of its genius for prudent compromise. It mingled Christian and heathen elements in the proportion suited to the taste of the age. It claimed to be simply conservative. In reality, it was very far from being anything of the kind. Its boasted organisation was a novelty: so was much of its teaching. It crushed out some principles of primitive Christianity, and put down more than one conservative reaction. At the same time it was certainly conservative, if we compare it with the revolutionary movements against which its early energies were in the main directed. Yet no small part of its skill was shown in wresting powerful weapons from its revolutionary foes, and turning these against their inventors.

## § 2. The extreme Intellectualism of the Gnostics.

The movement which, while it professed to turn Christianity into an intellectual system, would in the end have paralysed its strength as a religion, is known in history as Gnosticism. The Greek word *gnosis* means knowledge; the Gnostics were the men capable of knowledge, men who really understood divine things.

(1) The name was given in the first place to sects which arose in the east, and combined in a fanciful manner certain fragments of Judaism and Christianity with oriental forms of heathenism. Amalgamations of a similar character were in fashion before Christianity existed. Samaria with its mixed population and bastard Judaism was a very natural birth-place for religions of this sort, and there is no reason to doubt the truth of the early tradition that Simon the Samaritan Magician introduced a hybrid system, in which magical arts, Syrian and Phœnician mythology, were united with his own claims to be the Samaritan Messiah. In the later developments of Simon's doctrine by his disciples advantage was taken of Christian principles and of Christian terminology. Simon represented the supreme God, who under different names appears in all manifestations of the godhead. The divine 'thought' produced the angels. They in turn made the world, but they were ignorant of the Father and detained his Ennoia or 'thought' out of envy in the material universe. She underwent repeated incarnations, appearing for example as Helen of Troy, and as a woman of the same name who was a companion of Simon. At last the highest power revealed himself in Simon. He

came to seek 'the lost sheep,' to free his Ennoia or 'thought' from the fetters of matter, and at the same to deliver men by the knowledge which he conferred upon them. Simon had appeared among the Samaritans as the Father, among the Jews as the Son, among other nations as the holy Spirit. Cerinthus, who lived and taught in Asia Minor during the closing years of the first century, mingled Jewish and Christian elements with a theory which is foreign to both, viz.: that the world was not made by God but by inferior powers. Christ, a spirit who came from the supreme God, descended on Jesus at the moment of his baptism in the form of a dove, in order that Jesus who was merely a righteous man, born like his fellows, might be able to work miracles and reveal the unknown Father. Besides the Samaritan school of Simon and the Jewish school of Cerinthus, there was a cluster of oriental sects among whom the Ophites or Serpent-worshippers are conspicuous. They are Christian so far as this, that their mythology is coloured by Christian language and to some extent by a reverence for Jesus and by Christian thought. They are Gnostic, inasmuch as their mythology conveyed, under an allegorical form, the knowledge which taught men their state of bondage under matter and the means of deliverance from it.

(2) We have passed lightly over these early and eastern forms of Gnosticism. They had little direct influence on the history of the church, or on the development of its doctrine and institutions. But in the reign of Hadrian Gnosticism was transplanted to Alexandria, and from that moment began to exercise an immense influence, which continued during the whole of the second century.

In its Alexandrian or Greek form (for the culture of Alexandria was thoroughly Greek) Gnosticism is associated with two great names, those of Basilides and Valentinian. Each founded a school which counted numerous disciples in the west as well as in the east, and passed through various phases.

(3) The Greek Gnostics represent the same tendency which we have already noted in the Apologists. The gnosis or knowledge of which they made so much, was philosophical. The Fathers of the church who were its champions against Gnosticism, were not blind to the fact that the system which they opposed was indebted for its doctrines and its whole spirit to the philosophies of Pythagoras, Plato, Aristotle, and the Stoics. It is true that the Gnostics clothed their philosophic speculation in mythological garb, that they borrowed mysterious words from eastern languages, that they professed to purify the souls of their disciples by magical rites akin to those practised in the ancient mysteries, and in the mystical religions which were especially popular during the time of the Antonines. There is, however, clear proof that the Gnostics themselves attached a very subordinate importance to the details of this mythology. If the Gnostic systems appear to us in some respects magical and theosophic rather than philosophic, this only shows that the Gnostics were deeply imbued with the spirit of their age. Philosophy was tending to become theosophy, and so far as the Gnostics went beyond their time, they did but anticipate that fusion of philosophy with theosophy which manifested itself later in Neo-Platonism. Still, if the Apologists and Gnostics were alike philosophic Christians, the difference between them was very great.

The Gnostics carried to its utmost extreme the attempt to make Christianity philosophical. Again, their purpose was different. They were not explaining Christianity to persons who as yet knew little or nothing about it. They wished to make Christians understand their own religion. Philosophical speculation was, as they thought, the key which opened the hidden meaning of Christianity. It was the light which disclosed its true import and worth. It was almost inevitable that they should draw their disciples from the Christian congregations. Their adversaries taunted them with making it 'their whole 'business, not to convert heathen, but to subvert'[1] Christians.

### § 3. General Characteristics of Gnosticism.

Their endeavour was to find the deeper meaning of Christianity, its relation to other religions, and to the whole constitution of the universe. Such an attempt must come. But it could only be made by those who were already Christians (for how can a man reflect to any purpose on a religion with which he is not well acquainted?), by educated Christians, who were able to compare Christianity with the general knowledge of their time. The cause and effect are admirably stated by Origen. 'When ' men, not slaves and mechanics only, but also many from ' the educated classes in Greece, saw something venerable ' in Christianity, sects necessarily arose, not simply from ' love of strife and contradiction, but because many learned ' men strove to penetrate more deeply into the truths of

[1] Tertullian, *On Prescription*, 42.

'Christianity.'[1] We have now to enquire what conceptions were common to the different schools of Greek Gnosticism.

(1) They started from the Platonic principle of the opposition between matter and spirit. This principle has a superficial resemblance to the contrast between the flesh and the spirit, which is a cardinal point in the theology of St. Paul. The resemblance, however, is only superficial. St. Paul's distinction is chiefly moral. He speaks of a life 'according to the flesh' and another life 'according to the spirit.' It is the motives of conduct which distinguish the one life from the other. Externally they are the same. To Plato, and still more to the Gnostics, the distinction was metaphysical. The material world and contact with it were evil, or at least the unfailing source of imperfection and ignorance. From this principle the Gnostics inferred that God, *i.e.* the supreme and spiritual God, had not made the world which we see. From God they deduced a line of powers which emanated from Him, and were less and less perfect, as they were removed further and further from the ultimate source of being. At last one or several of these powers or angels had sunk into the depths of matter, and from this pre-existent matter had fashioned the material universe. In the constitution of human nature there are two elements. There is a spark of light in the human spirit, which has emanated from the spiritual God and been submerged in the gross, material world. And on the other hand this spark of light is confined not only in a material body, but also in a soul darkened by ignorance and error. The souls which are capable of better things beat the bars of the cage, but their struggle is in vain. At last Christ

[1] *Against Celsus*, iii. 12.

came from the sphere of heavenly light. He manifested that true and spiritual God previously unknown. He overcame the powers which ruled the world. By 'knowledge,' and by the institution of mystic rites, he freed those who are capable of salvation.

(2) It is easy to see that this theory involved an utter severance of all connection between Christianity and Judaism. Even allegorical methods of interpretation could hardly conceal the fact that the Hebrew Bible acknowledged one God, the Creator of heaven and earth. There had been a long controversy on the relations of the new religion to the old. The Gnostics settled the matter with relentless logic. They rejected the Jewish God and the Jewish Bible, then, be it remembered, the only Bible known to Christians. This was the way in which they vindicated the claim of Christianity to hold rank as the absolute religion. Further, as they continued to identify the Jewish God with the Creator, they really abandoned Monotheism. It is scarcely necessary to say that Monotheism was the tenet common to Judaism and to primitive Christianity, and that the controversy of the Apologists with the heathen turned in great measure on this very point. The Gnostics changed all that. They sacrificed Monotheism itself at the shrine of their Platonising philosophy.

(3) Having abandoned the Old Testament, the Gnostics sought for some other authority. They professed to find it in gospels, and in writings attributed to the Apostles. To some extent these writings were the same as those which were afterwards collected together and became authoritative among Christians generally, when they were known as the books of the new covenant, or, as we

THE GNOSTICS 153

now say, the New Testament. It is a significant fact that the interpretation of Christian documents began with the Gnostics. Basilides wrote an explanation of 'the gospel.' Heracleon penned the first commentary on the Gospel of St. John. Thus by their aversion to Judaism they inaugurated a new era, and that era continued long after the movement which gave it birth had perished; it continues still. They also appealed to the tradition which had been received by Apostolic men from the lips of Jesus, and handed down by them to others. But here, too, the Gnostics betrayed their radical and revolutionary spirit. Other Christians allegorised the Old Testament. But they accepted in their literal sense the facts of Christ's life, so far as they knew them. Nobody doubted that Jesus was really born, really died, really rose from the dead. A gospel or life of Jesus was esteemed for the story which it told. Even if some hidden meaning was found in Christ's actions, at all events the literal truth of the fact was also presupposed. The Gnostics took another line. They applied the same allegorical method which had long been allowed in the case of the Old Testament, to the facts of the Gospel history. These were the facts which had guided Christians in their allegorical interpretation of the Hebrew Scriptures. The Hebrew Scriptures had been tortured indeed, but still tortured according to one rule, definite so far, *viz.*: that they must be made to predict the facts of Christ's life, death, and resurrection. When these facts themselves were treated as allegories, the last barrier against arbitrary reconstruction was swept away. There was nothing to hinder the most complete transmutation of Christianity in the interests of Greek philosophy. Moreover, although Christians generally depended on tradition and on a tradition which was often far from trustworthy, they alleged well-known authorities, whose statements had been made publicly, if made at all, and could therefore be tested. The tradition of the Gnostics was by their own showing secret and esoteric: it had been handed down only to the initiated, and eluded every historical test.

(4) The Gnostics needed this license of interpretation, for their Platonic aversion to matter which had induced them to renounce belief in the Creator, compelled them also to transform the whole theory of redemption. St. Paul, though he believed Christ to be essentially a heavenly and pre-existent man, did not question the facts that he was 'born of a woman' and died on the Cross. The Gnostics could make no such admissions. If they were right, it was impossible that a being imprisoned in a material body should redeem others. How could he, seeing that he himself would stand in need of redemption? Christ was one of the æons or heavenly powers. He was no man but a spirit, one in his essence or nature with the Father. Either he united himself for a time with a wholly distinct being, the man Jesus, who was born and died, while Christ was incapable of human birth and death: or the body which Christ took was not of the same kind as ours: or finally, Christ's body was a mere phantom which deceived the eyes. Celsus, the heathen opponent of Christianity, tells us how Jesus should have lived and acted, had he been really equal to the claims made for him by his disciples. Some Gnostics altered the gospel history till it might very well satisfy the demands of Celsus. The offence of the cross was gone.

(5) For the old Christian hopes the Gnostics had no sympathy. We have shown above that the hope of a millenium died out, because the new environment was unfit to sustain it. To the Gnostics the thought of a millennial reign on earth would only have implied a prolongation of their imprisonment in matter. The Jewish colouring of the millennial dreams was to them simply contemptible. Not only so; but the belief in the resurrection of the body, which came from the Jews and which finally established itself in the Christian church, was contrary to the first principle of the Gnostics. Much more energetically than St. Paul did they believe that flesh and blood could not 'inherit the kingdom of God.'

(6) Gnostic Christianity had ceased to be a religion. It was before all things a theory of the universe, partly theosophical and fantastic, partly philosophical. It was not from sin but from matter and cosmical powers that man had to be delivered. It was not by faith or trust; it was not by good works; it was by knowledge, that deliverance came. The consequence was that Christianity, instead of being democratic, was dominated by an intellectual aristocracy. This aristocracy was one of birth. Only a limited number of men had within them that principle of light which could assimilate the light of Christ. These were the 'spiritual' men who alone could be saved in the full sense of the word. 'Hylic' men, *i.e.*, the creatures of matter, were doomed to destruction. 'Psychical' men, *i.e.*, those who had souls but had no spiritual nature, were capable of an imperfect bliss gained on the lower level of faith and good works. Salvation depended neither on man's free choice, nor on God's predestinating grace, but upon nature.

(7) At the same time a certain limited choice was open to spiritual natures. They were called upon to undergo a course of training, in order that the spiritual principle in them might be developed. This discipline was threefold. First it consisted in the acquirement of knowledge, which was taught like any other system of philosophy. Next, it implied ascetic life in the withdrawal, so far as might be, from material things, and in particular from the indulgence of the senses. Thirdly, the Gnostic was initiated in secret mysteries which purified the soul and were the pledge of eternal life. Sometimes these mysteries were no better than conscious jugglery. A Gnostic impostor called Marcus professed to change wine by his blessing into visible blood. The blood, he said, came from an æon or spiritual being called 'Grace,' and he gave it his disciples to taste.[1] But often, no doubt, these mystic initiations were taken in sober earnest, not only by those who were being initiated, but also by those who conducted the ceremonies. Mystical superstition, as we have had occasion to repeat, was not repulsive, but attractive to many among the educated classes of the day. One remark remains to be made before we dismiss this part of our subject. In describing Gnostic discipline with its philosophy, its asceticism, its mysteries, we have been taking it at the best. For theories on the evil of matter do not necessarily lead to rigorous abstinence. A man may argue that, if all contact with matter be evil, and if contact therewith be, as it is, inevitable, it is of no consequence what he does. He may come to think that licentiousness is, after all, no worse than eating and drinking. There were Gnostic sects in which such

[1] Irenæus, *Against Heresies,* i. 13, 2.

inferences were made, and in which the wildest excesses of debauchery were said to be encouraged.

§ 4. Marcion.

(1) One great and religious man, one of the greatest in the whole history of Christianity, is usually associated with Gnosticism. He has, indeed, much in common with it, though in other and most important points he stands apart. We refer to Marcion, who was born at Sinope, on the Black Sea, and, coming to Rome about 140, or a little later, taught and laboured there for many years. In some of his chief conclusions, he was at one with the Gnostics. Like them, he rejected the Hebrew Scriptures, which he interpreted in a Jewish sense, for, unlike most Christians of his time, he only recognised their plain and literal meaning. In true Gnostic fashion, he distinguished between two gods, one of them, the supreme Being, the other, the Creator of the world. He agreed with the most extreme among the Gnostics in contending that Christ's body was a mere phantom. Like many of the Gnostics, he imposed a life of severe mortification on his disciples, and he exhorted them to welcome martyrdom. But whereas the primary interest of the Gnostics was metaphysical, that of Marcion was religious. He was an ardent reformer, and his design was to purify Christianity from its corruptions by a criticism which distinguished its genuine elements from spurious additions. He carried this criticism back to the beginning. He took St. Paul as the standard of primitive purity, and charged the older Apostles with corrupting the gospel. Starting from

St. Paul's opposition between law and grace, he exaggerated this principle into the doctrine that the Jewish god, the creator, was a being of law and justice, good, but narrow and imperfect. Over against him stood the God of love, the God revealed in Christ. Christ was wholly different from the Jewish Messiah, who was to come from the creator, and had been predicted by his prophets. Marcion was by no means a consistent reasoner. The separation between abstract justice and love was seen to be hollow even by Marcion's opponents, and there is something ludicrous in a professed disciple of St. Paul's maintaining that there are two gods, and setting the authority of the Old Testament aside. Nevertheless, Marcion's power was great and far-reaching, and deservedly so. In the genuine spirit of religion he laid stress on faith, not on knowledge. He protested against the tendency which was rapidly spreading among Christians of Gnostic and of Anti-Gnostic opinions, the tendency to make their worship an imitation of heathen mysteries. In the churches which he founded, brotherly love, freedom from all ceremonies, and strict ascetic discipline, were the rule.

(2) Marcion was in all probability the first clearly to conceive the idea of a list or canon of Christian books, sacred and authoritative. For this purpose he selected the gospel according to St. Luke, purged it of alleged interpolations, and collected ten epistles of St. Paul, *i.e.*, all those which bear his name now, except the three pastoral epistles and the epistle to the Hebrews. His corrections, at least, as regards the gospel, were arbitrary in the extreme. Nevertheless, in his view of the relations between St. Paul and the older Apostles, Marcion laid

hold of a fact which has been the starting-point in the modern criticism of the New Testament. After his death a difference of principle between 'the holy Apostles' became utterly inconceivable to Christians. It is not too much to say that with Marcion, real insight into St. Paul's meaning died out among Christians, and never revived in the Catholic church. It is not without reason that Neander has spoken of Marcion as the Protestant of the ancient world.

(3) Marcion was at once the most dangerous rival of the older Christianity which he criticised, and of the new or Catholic Christianity which was being formed before his eyes. The weak points in his position were that like the Gnostics, he destroyed belief in one God, and like them, advocated belief in a god who was not the God of providence and of history. The Gnostics suffered from another and a fatal defect. With their exaltation of knowledge, they could found philosophical schools, and of these the world had enough; they could not found a church capable of uniting the learned and the simple, and that was what the world wanted. In opposition to Gnosticism, to supply the want which it failed to supply, to end the intolerable multiplication of sects in which the strength of Christianity spent itself in vain, 'the great church,' as it was sometimes called, the Catholic or Universal Church, as it was generally entitled, rose into being. Towards the close of the second century, the essential part of its construction was already complete. The rise of this great fabric must now be briefly described.

## CHAPTER VII.

### THE RISE OF THE CATHOLIC CHURCH.

(1) In the churches of the apostolic and sub-apostolic age, there were no officials, or at least, no officials to whom the duty of teaching was committed. The congregations were composed almost exclusively of simple and unlettered people, who were waiting in eager expectation for the second coming of Christ. There was, indeed, no lack of preaching. There were apostles who wandered from place to place, founded new churches, and exercised a natural authority over their converts. There were prophets to whom the mind and purpose of God was revealed, who announced what the Lord of the church demanded in the present, or was shortly to accomplish in his own person. There were teachers in the local congregations. The men, however, who exercised these various ministries, were neither chosen by the people or appointed by any human authority whatsoever. They held their commission directly from the divine spirit who moved them, who spoke in them, who manifested his presence by signs and wonders. Even the works of

mercy and the government of the flock were exercised spontaneously by persons who possessed the natural or supernatural qualifications, and who did not wait for any regular appointment. St. Paul speaks of 'those who have 'set themselves to minister unto the saints.' He mentions 'helps and governments' as supernatural gifts, as work for which, as we should now say, persons were marked out by the talents and means which God had given them.

(2) It was in this department of help and government that the first change occurred. A Christian congregation, viewed from one side, exactly answered to those benefit clubs which were common all over the Roman Empire. Now, a club requires officers to administer its funds, and to see that the rules of the club are kept. Further, a Christian congregation had to correspond at times with sister congregations, and to provide hospitable entertainment for Christians from other places. The early Christians had two patterns to follow. In the benevolent societies of the heathen world there were officers of administration and finance, often called *episkopoi* or 'overseers.' In the life-time of St. Paul, some Christians had adopted both the name and office, for he writes to the saints at Philippi, with the overseers or bishops and the deacons. The bishops administered the alms of the church, by which the love-feasts were provided and the poor relieved. The deacons or 'servants' assisted in the actual distribution. The other model present to the early Christians was that of the synagogue, in which discipline was administered by a council of presbyters or 'elders.' If, as there is some reason to think, the two boards of bishops and elders were originally distinct, they were at all

M

events soon amalgamated. A board of bishops or elders administered the finance and the discipline of the church, and they were assisted in the latter part of their duties by the deacons. But it must be carefully remembered that originally bishops or elders had, as such, nothing to do with the preaching of the word.

(3) After a time, two changes occurred which tended to increase the power of the bishops.

(*a*) The bishop or presbyter became a teacher. The enthusiasm of the first Christians had spent much of its force, and prophecy became rare. As genuine enthusiasm dies, hypocrisy is apt to take its place, and the prophetic gifts which still existed fell into discredit. But somebody must teach; if not an inspired teacher, then an official must instruct the congregation. It was natural to turn to the bishops, who with the deacons, were the only existing officials. It was also convenient that the same board which had the care of discipline, should also guard the purity of teaching. The two were intimately connected. When Gnostic teachers arose, the belief, the worship, the discipline of the congregation, were all imperilled. The chief care of instruction therefore fell to the bishops.

(*b*) Again, whereas at first the bishops or presbyters had been equal, the power of the whole board was gradually overshadowed by that of a permanent president, to whom the name of bishop or overseer was specially appropriated. He was expected to take advice from the rest of the board. But the president's position became distinctly superior to that of his colleagues. A church was no longer governed by a board of bishops and presbyters. It had one bishop as chief ruler and teacher. Under him stood the presbyters and the deacons. These changes occurred more slowly in some churches, more rapidly in others. The Ignatian epistles prove that they had been effected in the churches of Asia Minor, during the middle of the second century at latest. By the end of that century they had become universal.

(4) In ages when the creative faculty is strong, the critical faculty weak, people have short memories for the past. The monarchical power of the bishops began in the second century. Before that century was over, the belief prevailed that bishops were the successors of the apostles. Churches actually traced the line of their bishops back to the time of Peter or Paul. This succession of the bishops from the apostles, is the argument which Irenæus reiterates times without number against the Gnostics. 'We must obey' the bishops 'who have 'their succession from the apostles.'[1] Special importance in the controversy with heresy was given 'to the most ' ancient churches,'[2] which the apostles were said to have founded, and which were supposed to be the repositories of their teaching. Such was the church of Antioch: such was that of Alexandria: such was that of Rome, with its mythical foundation by the two 'most glorious apostles, ' Peter and Paul.' But apart from the supposed advantages of this kind, a bishop was supposed to have 'the ' grace of the truth,'[3] *i.e.*, a supernatural apprehension of it, which belonged to him by virtue of his office. Such a ' grace ' was attributed very naturally, and, in a sense, very rightly to the teachers of the apostolic age. They were appointed by a direct call from God, and they spoke

---
[1] Irenæus, *Against Heresies,* iv. 26, 2.
[2] Irenæus, iii. 4, 1.   [3] Irenæus, iv. 26, 2 and 5.

'as the spirit gave them utterance.' When the monarchical bishops became the chief teachers, the *charisma* or grace proper to the inspired was claimed by the bishop, who, of course, stood on a totally different footing.

### § 2. The world-wide Federation of the Bishops.

In the Ignatian epistles, much as they exalt the monarchical power of the bishop, attention is chiefly fixed on the local church. It is there that the bishop rules in the place of Christ, and his power does not extend further. But when the episcopate came to be regarded as the continuation of the apostolic college, the bishops were both in thought and in fact associated together. The bishops of neighbouring cities met in council to defend their common interests against doctrines or usages which were prejudicial to them.

(1) Thus the bishop was no longer merely the officer of a particular congregation. He held office in an aristocratic confederation which secured unity of belief throughout the known world, and this confederation of bishops with the inferior clergy and laity was called the Catholic or universal church. A man who chose his own belief was branded as a heretic, and the name of itself implied condemnation. More and more, union with this Catholic church was made the indispensable condition of salvation. Cyprian, who was bishop of Carthage in the middle of the third century, maintains that even agreement with the bishops in the orthodox faith is not enough. In his view it does not matter much what a man teaches, 'so long as he teaches outside of the

'church : whoever and whatsoever he may be, he is no 'Christian, who is not in the church of Christ.'[1] 'He 'cannot have God for his father, who has not the church 'for his mother.'[2] The influence of the Roman Empire had completely changed the whole idea of the church. In apostolic times the church did not pretend to furnish the means of salvation. Salvation came directly from God, and those who were already saved constituted the church. The church, too, was an ideal body, the reflection of 'the church of the first-born who are enrolled in heaven.' It was cemented by invisible forces, by faith, by hope, by love. But the church of the third century was a political confederation, which reflected, not a heavenly ideal, but the civil constitution of the Roman Empire. The bishops were its magistrates: it was an empire within an empire: its officers were elected by ordinary human means, and often rivalled the governors of provinces in love of power, of pomp, and even of wealth. It only wanted a visible head instead of the invisible Christ, to make the parallel with the Roman Empire perfect.

(2) This final change was not brought about in the first three centuries of the church, but even then there were premonitory symptoms of it. Although the bishops were all rulers of the church, the bishops of the third century were by no means equal either in law or in fact. The order of their primacy and subordination followed the natural divisions of the Empire. The bishop of the chief town in a province frequently possessed the right of convoking the bishops of the province, and presiding at

[1] Cyprian, *Letters*, v. 24.
[2] *On the Unity of the Catholic Church*, 6.

their meeting. He had also a voice in the nomination of bishops throughout the province. The power of the bishop of Alexandria, the second city in the Empire, extended, not only over Egypt, but also over Libya and Pentapolis; the bishop of Carthage exercised a primacy over Numidia and the two Mauretanias, as well as over Proconsular Africa. But the power of the Roman bishop was already beginning to overshadow the Roman world. The Roman church was the church of the metropolis of the world; its wealth enabled it to relieve poorer churches even in distant regions; it possessed the Roman tact for government, and anticipated measures of consolidation which other churches adopted more slowly. It boasted of its foundation by the two great Apostles, just as the city traced its origin to the two mythical heroes Romulus and Remus; and in the west it was the only church surrounded with the halo of apostolic origin. All these circumstances tended to make the vote of the Roman bishop decisive in controversy. 'With this church,' says Irenæus, 'every 'church must agree because of its more powerful 'principality.'[1] The Roman bishop Victor, at the end of the second century, 'tried to cut off the dioceses of all 'Asia from the common union,'[2] because they differed from him about the celebration of Easter. A little later we find the Roman bishop Callistus establishing his pretensions on the ground of Christ's promise to Peter, 'On this rock I will build my church; ... I will give 'unto thee the keys of the kingdom of heaven.' Tertullian, who had a quarrel with Callistus, calls him mockingly 'the bishop of bishops, the chief pontiff,' (a title assumed

---

[1] Irenæus, *Against Heresies*, iii. 3, 2.
[2] Eusebius, *Eccl. Hist.* v. 24, 9.

by the Roman Emperor) and speaks of his 'peremptory edict.'[1] Cyprian acknowledges in the Roman church 'the chair of Peter,' 'the chief church whence the unity 'of the priesthood (*i.e.* of the episcopate) had its origin.'[2] A very uncritical use has been often made of these facts by Roman Catholic controversialists. They fall far short of proof that the Roman primacy was acknowledged definitely and consistently in the church of the third century. Cyprian, for example, had no fixed princples to guide him on the relations of the Roman bishop to the rest of the episcopate. He acknowledged the primacy of Rome, and stoutly maintained the equality of all bishops, just as it suited him. Nevertheless the foundations of the Roman primacy were already laid. A new church had arisen which claimed to be the church of Christ and his Apostles, while it had in fact replaced that church by a political organisation. In an age later than that with which we have to deal, the Roman bishop replaced the Roman Emperor. At last, in the middle ages and in the western world, the words 'Roman' and 'Catholic,' long connected, became identical in meaning, and the organisation of the Catholic church was perfected.

---

[1] Tertullian, *On Modesty*, 1 and 21.
[2] Cyprian, *Letters*. lix. 14.

## § 3. The Work of the New Church.

The organisation which has just been described, was not solely or even chiefly the creation of ambitious or self-seeking men. It succeeded because it answered to a real want, and saved Christianity from a great danger. That danger was, as has been already said, occasioned by the Gnostics. The confederation of bishops stemmed the flood of Greek speculation, when it was on the point of sweeping away those positive beliefs which were the distinctive mark of Christianity.

(1) The first great work of the new church with its episcopal organisation consisted in establishing and imposing a 'rule of faith.' This 'rule of faith,' this 'canon or rule of the truth,' for it was called by various names, was an expansion of the form used in baptism. Not indeed of the oldest form, since at first converts were baptised 'in the name of Jesus Christ.' But from the middle of the second century, and possibly from an earlier date, it was the prevailing, though not the universal custom to baptise 'into the name of the Father and of the 'Son and of the Holy Spirit.' This later form which had arisen from the threefold benediction with which St. Paul closes his second epistle to the Corinthians, was expanded by the Fathers who conducted the controversy with the Gnostics, into a simple and compendious summary of Christian belief. The orthodox Christian was required to profess his belief in the one God who had created all things, in Jesus Christ the Son of God, who had been born miraculously, had suffered and died, risen again and ascended into heaven, whence he would

come to judge mankind, and finally to profess belief in the Holy Spirit. This rule of faith was perpetually in the mouths of orthodox controversialists. It was their boast that they held fast 'the immovable rule of the truth 'which they had received through baptism.'[1] They professed to have received it by unbroken tradition from the Apostles, and this rule (with a few later additions) is still familiarly known as the 'Apostles' creed.' The proof of its apostolic origin was furnished by the agreement of the churches all the world over, and above all by the consent of those churches which had been founded by the Apostles themselves, and could trace back the succession of their bishops in unbroken line to them. A public tradition was used to counteract the secret tradition of Gnostic wisdom. Universal consent and unswerving continuance in the truth were contrasted with the many sects and constant flux of Gnostic opinion, and, so contrasted, they overpowered the imagination of ordinary Christians. The fallacy of the Catholic argument lies on the surface. It assumes that the Apostles founded the confederation of bishops, the political organisation which called itself the Catholic church. It assumes that the belief of the churches never changed. It assumes that the Apostles had handed down a formula of faith. All three assumptions were made in the teeth of history. Nevertheless, by contrast with the belief of the Gnostics, and of Marcion, that there were two gods, and that there was no organic connection between the revelation made through the Hebrew prophets and that which was given in Christ, the Catholic 'rule of faith' was moderate, conservative, and by comparison Apostolic.

[1] Irenæus, *Against Heresies*, i. 9, 4.

(2) In his conflict with the Christians who maintained the 'rule of faith' Marcion had a powerful weapon in his hands. If the ordinary Christian could appeal to the tradition of the Apostolic churches, Marcion could appeal with better reason to the Apostolic writings, to 'the Gospel' and to 'the Apostle,' *i.e.* to ten Pauline epistles. The orthodox churches had not the same advantage. Marcion rejected the Hebrew Bible and had instead a Bible of his own, which even his opponents could not afford to contemn. Accordingly the churches which were forming themselves into the great Catholic confederation, began to draw up a list of Christian writings which covered Marcion's list and overlapped it. These writings in respect of authority and inspiration were now put on a level with the Old Testament. Here was a change scarcely less remarkable than the rise of the Catholic hierarchy. As late as the middle of the second century a New Testament did not exist. By this we do not of course mean that the documents which form our present New Testament, were written after that time. Most of them are much older, and several of the epistles which bear St. Paul's name are undoubtedly authentic. But these writings were not collected together and put forward as of decisive authority for faith and practice. The early Christians built their faith on the Old Testament with its supposed predictions of Jesus Christ, on the sayings of Jesus as handed down by oral or written tradition, on the sayings or writings of Christian prophets. Written records of the life and sayings of Jesus were highly valued: they were read, as we learn from Justin, in the Christian meetings—but they were valued only so far as they were believed to be accurate reports. It is only the books of the Old

Testament which Justin mentions as inspired, and which he quotes with such formulæ as 'The Holy Spirit saith.' Only one exception has to be made. He quotes 'the 'revelation made to John,'[1] for while to him Christian histories and Christian epistles had no definite authority, Christian prophecy had. But within fifty years from Justin's time a notable change had occurred. This change is best expressed in the words of Tertullian, 'the church mingles the law and the prophets with the 'evangelical and the apostolic literature: thence she 'drinks in her faith.'[2] Thus while the oldest Christianity canonised the Old Testament, while Marcion canonised a New Testament, the Catholic church canonised both, and at the same time enlarged Marcion's list. A formal list of New Testament writings is given in a document known as the Muratorian canon, which represents the view of the Roman church in the last part of the second century. A similar list is implied in the writings of Irenæus, who may be taken as the spokesman of Gaul and Asia Minor, and in Tertullian, who testifies to current opinion in Africa and Rome. As yet the list was by no means fixed and closed. Centuries elapsed before all the books of our modern New Testament were included, and all the books which form no part of our New Testament excluded. Again, there are indications that the churches of Rome and Asia Minor anticipated the other churches in the formation of the canon. Nevertheless, the divine authority of the four gospels, of thirteen Pauline epistles, of the Acts of the Apostles, of the first epistles of St. Peter and St. John, obtained general recognition during the course of the third century.

[1] Justin, *Dialogue*, 81.  [2] Tertullian, *On Prescription*, 36.

(3) This fundamental change was closely connected with that rise of the hierarchy which was more or less contemporaneous with it. In each case the change was possible because the enthusiasm, the sense of present inspiration, had died out among Christians. When the Montanists of Phrygia tried to revive prophetical gifts, and to settle the discipline of the church by the inspired utterances of their prophets, the spread of the movement in the church at large was checked by the general conviction that revelation had been completed once and for all in the Apostolic records. At the same time the germ of the New Testament which had been dangerous in the hands of Marcion became harmless to the Catholic church, when enlarged and linked to the Old Testament. There was no longer any possibility of that 'blasphemy 'against the Creator' which had shocked Christian feeling in Marcion. No doubt, St. Paul's epistles afforded ready means of criticising the hierarchical church, and in ages still far distant they were destined to shake that church to its foundation. But in the meantime their force was neutralised by their juxtaposition with other writings of a different cast, and by the accepted theory that the Apostles and indeed all the scriptural writers were unanimous, because all were alike inspired. Of course it was also taken for granted that 'the rule of faith' and the Bible were in absolute harmony. Tradition was not supposed to supplement scripture. This is the view taken by Roman Catholics, but it was not the view of the old Catholic church. The old Catholic belief was that Scripture gave at greater length, with greater fulness, but also in a form more liable to misinterpretation, the truth which was stated more briefly and also more clearly in the traditional rule of faith.

## § 4. Growth of Speculative Theology.

Things, however, could not rest here, and the 'rule of faith' was in the end deeply affected by the authority of the New Testament.

(1) Originally, 'the rule of faith' was a rampart raised against the Gnostics. The candidate for baptism had to profess his belief in 'God the Father Almighty,' to which, for the sake of greater clearness, some churches added the words, ' maker of heaven and earth.' This is neither more nor less than monotheism, which, among the Hebrews, at least, had arisen quite independently of philosophy. The rest of the creed is concerned with matters of fact and not of speculation. Jesus is called 'the Son of God,' a title afterwards qualified by the addition of 'only-begotten.' The 'Son of God,' however, is a title borrowed by the first Christians from the Hebrew Bible, and it had at first no metaphysical meaning. The 'rule of faith' has nothing to say about the deity of Christ. It does not even speak of him as the Word, or assert his pre-existence before his human birth. But by the acceptance of the gospel and first epistle attributed to St. John, the Catholic church pledged itself to the belief that Christ was the pre-existent Word of God. And not only so. It was obliged to look upon this doctrine as part of the faith handed down by the apostles.

(2) A new impetus was thus necessarily given to those philosophical speculations which had begun with the Gnostics on the one hand, and with the Apologists on the other. A multitude of difficult questions forced themselves upon the attention of educated and thoughtful

Christians. If Christ was God, and the Father was God the Almighty Creator, how was it that the church asserted so strenuously the divine unity? If Christ was begotten of the Father, and was the instrument of creation, when did this spiritual birth take place? From eternity, or in the moment which preceded the creation? In what sense was Christ one with the Father, and in what sense distinct from him? Many discordant answers were given to these urgent questions. Not that they were felt to be urgent by all. The bulk of Christians, had they been let alone, would have been satisfied with the old belief in one God the Father, and would have distrusted 'the dispensation,' as it was called, by which the sole deity of the Father expanded itself into the deity of the Father and the Son. To this aversion Tertullian bears strong, because unwilling witness. 'All simple people,' he writes, 'not to call them ignorant and uneducated, (and these 'always form the greater part of believers) since the rule '[of faith] itself transfers them from the many gods of the 'world to the only true God, take fright at the dispensa-'tion. They take for granted that the number and 'arrangement of the Trinity is a division of the unity. 'They will have it that we are proclaiming two or three 'Gods. We, say they, hold the rule of One.'[1]

(3) It became, however, more and more clear that the old belief in the sole godhead of the Father was no longer tenable in the church. There were a certain number of persons in Asia Minor at the close of the second century known as *Alogoi*, *i.e.*, persons who did not receive the doctrine of a personal Word. But they were of little account, because they consistently rejected

[1] Tertullian, *Against Praxeas*, 3.

the fourth gospel, the authority of which was already beyond question in the church. Theodotus, the Tanner, who came to Rome about 190, met with no better success. He was a man of learning who founded a school in which a dry and rationalistic interpretation of the Scriptures went hand in hand with the study of mathematics and logic, of Euclid and Aristotle. But when he denied that Jesus was anything more than a righteous man under the special influence of the divine Spirit, he found that the general feeling of the Christian world was too strong for him, and the Roman bishop, Victor, drove him from the communion of the church.

(4) A movement which assumed various phases classified under the general name of Sabellianism, seemed to have a better chance of holding its ground in the church. According to the oldest phase of this doctrine, which was favoured by three successive bishops of Rome, Christ is absolutely identical with the Almighty Father: it is the Father himself who was born and who died. Thus monotheistic belief and the glory due to Christ both remained in their integrity. According to later developments of this theory (and Sabellius himself was one of its latest advocates) God is named Father, Son, and Holy Spirit, in virtue of the three 'masks' or characters under which He is known. But the theology which made a real distinction between the absolute God who transcends all being and all thought, and the Logos or Word through whom He creates and governs the world, and through whom He reveals himself, was too deeply rooted in the philosophical tendencies of the age to suffer displacement. It was upheld by the genius and learning of Origen, who is the father of that theological system which, not indeed

without serious emendation, became the accepted theology of the church.

(5) The last desperate effort to render the belief in the divine unity consistent and real was made by Paul of Samosata, who became bishop of Antioch in 260. He admitted that the Logos, by which he understood chiefly the attribute of divine wisdom, dwelt in Christ. The divine wisdom, however, did not become incarnate in Jesus. His personality was human : he was morally, not essentially, one with God. The wisdom which came from God was a quality of his soul, and was imparted to him, as to the prophets and to Moses, but in a higher degree. Three great synods were held to examine the doctrine of the bishop of Antioch, and only in the third, which met in 268, was he formally condemned. The history of the dispute is singularly instructive. Paul practically acknowledged the hold of the Logos doctrine on the church by retaining the term, while he emptied it of its meaning. Next, his chief antagonist was Malchion, a sophist of Antioch, and president of a learned school in that city. Thirdly, Paul exhibits the secular spirit which had invaded the church. He was a kind of viceroy, under Zenobia, the eastern queen, who was for a time mistress of Antioch. It was to her protection that he trusted in his quarrel, and when in 272 Antioch again became part of the empire, Paul of Samosata fell with the queen, whose cause he had espoused. He refused to surrender the ecclesiastical buildings. Thereupon his opponents appealed to the Emperor, Aurelian, who decided that they belonged of right to that party ' with which the Christian bishops of Italy and of Rome were in correspondence.'[1] The unity of the church

---

[1] Eusebius, *Eccl. Hist.* vii. 30.

depended on the unity of the empire. The church was a political corporation in which the bishops were the magistrates, and among those magistrates a preponderant authority was assigned by the Emperor to the bishops of Italy, and in particular to the bishop of Rome, the metropolis of the world.

(6) From the time of the controversy with Paul of Samosata the speculative theology of Origen was embodied in the chief eastern churches. What had been then theology now ranked as religion, and as a matter of course, the philosophical dogmas identified but yesterday with the Christian faith were said to be apostolic. In the west there was less taste for speculative theology, and the simpler creed which protected Christian monotheism against the Gnostics sufficed. But even in the west the Roman bishop, Dionysius (259-269), could write 'Sabellius blasphemes, alleging the Son himself to be the Father,'[1] and Cyprian summarily dismisses the doctrine that it was the Father who suffered, as one of the 'heretical plagues.'[2] At the end of our period, the basis of Christian union had been completely changed. It consisted no longer in the same trust, the same hope, the same aspirations after holiness of life, the same allegiance to a common Lord. To be a Christian, a man must give intellectual assent to an elaborate series of philosophical propositions. The new creed was as yet in the germ. In the centuries which follow, chiefly in the fourth and fifth, the church was occupied in perfecting it. Political intrigue and the confusion of political with religious motives, the principle that the

[1] Routh, *Rell. Sacr.* iii. p. 373.
[2] Cyprian, *Letters*, lxxiii. 4.

bishops were to decide the belief of the laity, and that the opinions of individual bishops were to follow the vote of the majority, bodily pains and penalties inflicted in case of resistance, were among the evils which accompanied the new order of things.

### § 5. Christian Mysteries.

Throughout the course of its development in the second and third centuries, the Catholic church profited by the example of the Gnostics. It arose in opposition to them, but also adopted much that was important from their principles and practice. This is just what might have been expected. The Gnostics devised a mixed system, partly Greek, partly Christian. The Catholic church set itself the same task, but it did slowly, cautiously, and with moderation, that which the Gnostics did recklessly and in haste. Like the Gnostics, the church ended by making philosophic theory and intellectual conviction the basis of union, although the Catholics were much more conservative in their treatment of Christianity as an historical and positive religion, and made philosophical speculation safe by committing it to the superintendence of the bishops, who had the capacity for government and the instinct of the statesman for practical compromise.

(1) There was another way in which the course taken by the church resembles the example given by the Gnostics. The Catholic worship became more and

more a close imitation of the mysteries popular in the Roman Empire.[1]

(a) The convert was introduced to the full membership of the church by a baptismal rite which was already surrounded with mystery and pomp. He solemnly renounced the devil and his works: in some cases he was exorcised: the water was consecrated: the forehead, the ears, the nostrils, and the breast were anointed with oil: the imposition of hands was supposed to convey the Holy Spirit, after the water had washed away sin. Milk and honey were put into the mouth of the new Christian. He was clothed in a white robe, which he continued to wear for some time. Instead of being proclaimed on the house-tops, Christianity came to be regarded as a mysterious system, with secrets which it was sacrilege to reveal, except to the initiated, *i.e.*, the baptised. It was only to the earlier and less solemn part of the worship that the catechumens were admitted. The Greek mysteries culminated in 'the contemplation' of the

---

[1] Justin, *First Apology*, 66 compares the Eucharist with 'the mysteries of Mithra.' Tertullian, *Apol.* 7, *Against the Nations*, 7, implies that 'silence faithfully maintained is due to all mysteries,' and therefore to the secrets of the Christian assemblies. This is probably the first notice of the 'discipline of the secret,' as it came to be called. In much earlier times (*Coloss.* i. 26, Ignatius, *To the Ephes.* 12, comp. Clement of Alexandria, *Exhortation*, 12, *Miscellanies*, iv. 25. vi. 15) 'mystery' and the allied words had been adopted into the Christian vocabulary. But the notion of secrecy was absent. A mystery meant something once hidden, but now revealed, *viz.*: in Christ. Thus the word 'mystery' was used first of Christian teaching, then of Christian ceremonies: finally the bond of secrecy was superadded and the knowledge of the mysteries reserved to the initiated, *i.e.*, the baptised.

most sacred symbols. The Christian mysteries culminated in the Eucharist.

(*b*) Almost from the beginning, a superstitious element intruded itself into the Eucharist rite. In the Ignatian epistles, the Eucharist is said to be 'the antidote against death,' 'the medicine of immortality,'[1] and immortality was the very gift which the Eleusinian mysteries professed to impart. The church of the first three centuries had no fixed doctrine on the Eucharist, but the consecrated elements were believed on all hands to be the channels of mysterious grace. They were sent to the sick and to prisoners, taken in private before other food, even by those who had attended the celebration of the mysteries, given in the eastern and African churches to baptised infants. This last practice of giving communion to infants shows the magical character which the Eucharist had assumed. Like infant baptism, which became customary in the western church during the third century, infant communion was, by the necessity of the case, a magical or mystical rite, which was thought to convey a spiritual blessing in the total absence of moral or intellectual dispositions.

(2) The institution of the Christian priesthood was the crown of this mystical tendency. In apostolic times, all Christians were priests, and the sacrifices offered were the sacrifices of prayer and of self-surrender to God. Afterwards, the gifts furnished by the members of a congregation and consumed partly in the Eucharist, partly in love-feasts, partly in the support of the poor, were viewed as a sacrifice offered to God. This sacrifice, however, was offered by the whole congregation, and the presiding

[1] Ignatius, *To the Ephesians*, 20.

officers simply spoke and acted in their name. Later still, when mystical conceptions of the Eucharist were pervading the church, the notion of a Christian priesthood was still in abeyance. The word 'priest' is used of Christian officers by Tertullian and Origen, but the former laid no stress on the strict meaning of the word; the latter uses it tentatively and almost with an apology. Cyprian, on the other hand, was quite in earnest about the Christian priesthood, and had the courage of his convictions. According to him, the bishop is God's priest, whose office it was 'to serve the altar and celebrate 'divine sacrifices,' and the sacrifice which he offers is 'the passion of the Lord.' The priesthood, once acknowledged, could scarcely fail to become the central point in the functions and dignity of the bishop. It is as priest that the bishop teaches and guards the purity of doctrine: as priest that he exercises the power of the keys and bestows or withholds divine grace. He is not really the successor of Christ and the apostles, or even of the Jewish priest. The analogies of Jewish worship were used to support and extend the power of the Christian priesthood, but the origin of the Christian priesthood was not derived from Judaism. It first appears in Gentile churches and among the Gnostics, who rejected the Old Testament in its entirety. It is an inheritance from the religion of the Empire, and the hierophant in the heathen mysteries is the prototype of the Christian priest.

## § 6. The Relaxation of Discipline.

It would be quite unfair to charge the Catholic church in its early days with concentrating the whole of its attention on doctrine and mystical rites. During the whole of our period it maintained what would now be thought an extreme rigour of moral discipline. Nevertheless, the church was already obliged to abate the severity of its rules, and accommodate itself to its environment in the Roman world.

(1) At first, great sins, such as murder, immorality, and lapse into idolatry, excluded a baptised member of the church from its communion for the rest of his life. In Spain, this discipline, as appears from the acts of the synod of Elvira, continued as late as the beginning of the fourth century. Elsewhere, more consideration was shown to human weakness. The Montanists, who were conservative in their maintenance of the old discipline, as well as of the ancient prophetical office, protested against the laxity of the Roman bishop (Zephyrinus or Callistus), who readmitted adulterers to the communion of the church. Special difficulties were caused by the unpredecented severity of the Decian persecution. The number of apostates was great. It seemed impossible to leave them all outside the church when persecution was still raging, and the apostates, exposed to the danger of a fresh fall, needed all the strength that could be given them. Cyprian, by nature a rigorist, listened to the supplication of the confessors, accepted the 'letters of peace' which they gave to their fallen brethren, and restored the latter, if ready to do penance, to the communion of the

church. Cornelius, the Roman bishop, took the same course, and even communicated with bishops who had offered sacrifice to idols. Again a vigorous protest was made. Novatian, one of the Roman presbyters, argued that the church by professing to forgive deadly sins anticipated the judgment of God, and forfeited its own character, as the 'church of the pure.' Novatian had a strong party with him, and he had powerful adherents, such as Fabian, bishop of Antioch. But time was on the side of the milder practice, and of the hierarchical principles which put the power of absolution in the hands of the bishops. Novatian and his followers were driven out, and formed a Puritan sect. The church which expelled them was on its way to become a mixed body, which by its own confession included the goats as well as the sheep, and shut its doors not against sinners but against heretics.

(2) Besides these reactions against the increasing and inevitable corruption of a church which aspired to be the church of the whole Empire, there was a reaction which held its place within the church, and which exercised a momentous and enduring influence. As the church in general was sinking to a lower plane of morality, the perfect life, as understood in an age which made a false opposition between matter and spirit, was exhibited in its integrity by the ascetics, who abstained from flesh-meat and wine, and from marriage, and devoted themselves to prayer and contemplation. They were already forming themselves into communities. The time was near when the deserts of Egypt and Syria were to be peopled by solitaries. In a sense, monachism was a reaction against the hierarchy. The dignity of the

bishop depended on his office and his magical powers. That of the monk, who was at first a layman, depended on the sanctity of his life. Monasticism, with all its faults, saved Christianity from the complete domination of the priesthood, and preserved the memory of a religion which was not of the world. When the two streams of monachism and sacerdotalism flowed together, the monks improved the general tone of the priesthood. But these considerations belong to the history of the middle ages rather than to that of the first three centuries.

# CHAPTER VIII.

## IMPENDING TRIUMPH OF THE MIXED SYSTEM.

THE heading of this chapter will not, it is hoped, need much justification to the reader who has followed us thus far. Christianity, if by Christianity we mean the spiritual religion of Jesus in its unadulterated simplicity, never did triumph over the empire. It is not the religion of the world, or of any part of the world, even now. Constantine is reckoned the first Christian Emperor, and the courtly prelate Eusebius thought no flattery too much for a ruler who had given first peace, and then wealth and power, to the church. When, however, we remember that the Emperor put the sign of the cross on his banner and bore it on his helmet, we may well ask whether his religious zeal would have satisfied Jesus, as it satisfied Eusebius. To a certain extent the principles of Jesus did enter into the future history of civilization. The world is very different from what it would have been without the life and death of Christ. But the system which became the religion of the empire borrowed one half of its contents from the empire which it overcame. We have seen how heathen morality, philosophy, and superstition, helped to make it what it was and is. Moreover, this mixed system won its way slowly, not without the aid of the secular arm. Two centuries and more had to pass before its victory was complete even in the cities. When Benedict, the father of western monachism, went to Monte Cassino in 529, he found himself in the midst of a population which worshipped Venus and Apollo. In the same year Justinian was driving the remnant of heathen magistrates, physicians, and philosophers from Constantinople, and dispatching a bishop to the neighbouring provinces in Asia, where he baptised seventy thousand Pagans. Still, if the full triumph of Christianity was deferred for two hundred years after the close of the third century, that triumph was already assured before Constantine ascended the throne. The members of the church were far outnumbered by the heathen population of the empire. But the church was the one living and growing power in the empire. The persecuting Emperors practically acknowledged their defeat, when, sorely against their will, they laid down the sword. Indeed, Maximin publicly stated that 'nearly everybody had abandoned 'the worship of the gods and attached themselves to the 'Christian people.'[1] This is the language of rhetorical exaggeration. But it proves the Emperor's sense of the power which the church possessed.

---

[1] Eusebius, *Eccl. Hist.* ix. 9.

§ 1. Foreign Elements brought into Christianity.

In examining the causes which made Christianity the religion of the future, we may begin with those which were due to the accretions foreign to the religion of Jesus.

(1) The religion of Jesus was, the religion of the Catholic church was not, too lofty for the generality of mankind. The latter accommodated itself to the people with whom it had to deal. Much of the change was made in no ignoble spirit. The theologians adopted the best morality they knew from the philosophers of the time. The Christian ascetics recalled the best features in Stoicism, and Galen, who was moved to special admiration, not only by the courage with which Christians met death, but also by the ascetic impulse which induced many of them to lead a single life, was fain to confess that in the government of their passions and in eager pursuit of virtue 'they reached a pitch which true philosophers 'could not out-do.'[1] Something has been said above on the mischievous effects of asceticism, but this does not alter the fact that it was attractive to the best spirits of the empire. So too, the metaphysical theorising which repels us, was welcome in the early ages of the church. Theologians, of whom Origen is the chief, were occupied partly in translating the original ideas of Christianity into the language of the philosophic schools, partly in appropriating the ideas of Greek philosophy and giving them a place and a home in the belief of the church.

(2) Again the rhetoric of the Greeks was continued in

[1] The passage is given at length by Harnack, *Dogmengeschichte*, i. p. 170.

the Christian homily. For on that department also, Greek influence told. A studied oration carefully prepared beforehand replaced the extempore effusions of the prophets, who spoke in ecstasy. We are apt to find the rhetoric of Christian orators wanting in simplicity and directness, but the tricks of rhetoric were the fashion of the time, which was very unlike the time of Aeschines and Demosthenes. The more enlightened among the Christians had no mind to forego the advantages to be got from a study of classical literature, and Julian well knew that he was aiming a heavy blow at the new religion when he closed the Christian schools of grammar and rhetoric, and confined Christian teachers to the exposition of the gospels in the churches of the Galileans.

(3) Add to this that the Christians were strong because the federation of bishops, which ruled the church, made them one. The empire was divided by faction. After the reign of the Antonines it had no principle of stability. The old Roman state had been protected by religious sanctions. In the mingling of nations, a religion which was either national or else nothing, lost its hold, and the empire was left defenceless. It created no enthusiasm: it was a prey to the violence and greed of the soldiery: it was beginning to fail before the barbarous hordes of the north. In contrast with an empire undermined and tottering, the church was stable, and claimed a divine authority, which gained credence and in which men were to believe for ages to come. The church came to the rescue of the empire which had striven to exterminate it. The gain to the empire was not pure gain. After a time, the forces of the eastern empire were drained by the insane fury of dogmatic strife, and

the Moslem hosts were devastating the fairest provinces of the empire, while its subjects were disputing whether Christ had two wills or one. All this should be frankly acknowledged. But it should also be remembered that in the west the church was the school in which the Teutonic nations learnt the civilisation of ancient Rome, and the blurred traditions of Greek philosophy. When the Renaissance brought the treasures of Greek literature to light, it could do little direct work for religion. The Catholic religion had long ago incorporated, and still preserved, the elements of Greek philosophy and ethics. It has been noticed with surprise that Barberini, an orthodox cardinal of the seventeenth century, warmly appreciated the meditations of Marcus Aurelius. There is no cause for astonishment in this. The morality of the Stoics had been adapted to the use of the church fourteen centuries before by Clement of Alexandria. The apparent coincidence of Catholic and Stoic morality simply arises from their identity, from the fact that the morality of Jesus and of Paul had been rejected to make room for the morality of the Porch.

(4) The church made another concession, which was directly addressed to the weakness of the human mind. It fostered the craving for magical rites, and in the end came to terms with polytheism. This tendency was still in its initial stage. But we have seen the magical virtue attributed almost from the first to baptism and the Eucharist, and the process by which Christian rites were fashioned on the model of the Greek and oriental mysteries. Magical superstition was to attain colossal proportions in the church, In the fourth century relics of the martyrs, the pages of the gospels, the consecrated

elements of the Eucharist, fragments of the true cross, were highly valued as amulets, which drove off demons, and guarded the wearer from every kind of spiritual and bodily hurt. Not very much later a crowd of martyrs and saints occupied the vacant place which had once been tenanted by gods and heroes. The office of the one and the other was the same. They were the patrons to whom men looked for health, for safety on journeys, for the blessing of children, for the satisfaction, in a word, of all their desires.

### § 2. Intrinsic Strength of Christianity.

(1) Such were the accommodations, some noble, some ignoble, by which the church adapted itself to circumstances and was fitted to become the religion of the empire. But accommodation cannot wholly explain the triumph of the Catholic church. If it took very much from the empire, it had also very much to bestow upon the empire. The plant grows by assimilating elements from the soil, but there can be no growth without that principle of life which lies hid within the seed. So it was with the Catholic church. It had a principle of life which did not come from Greek or Roman civilisation, but from the religion of Jesus. It was because of this that it overcame the Roman world. It won the day, not merely because it skilfully turned old elements to its advantage, but also because it introduced new principles. Adaptation was the condition, but its originality was the true cause of its success. With a consideration of this originality we shall conclude this chapter and this book.

(2) In the first place Christianity was, and through all its phases remained, much more than a system of speculation. The 'Apostles' creed,' which is intended to be a record of fact, never ceased to be valued, and even the longer and later creeds, which go by the names of Nicene and Athanasian, mingle the facts of history with metaphysical dogma. This was the secret of the church's strength. Of mere speculation the world was tired. Philosophy had done its utmost. It had reduced the old belief in gods many and lords many, to belief in one great power which sustains the universe.[1] It had given an ethical character to religion: it insisted that a virtuous life was the one thing needful, and relegated sacrifice and ritual to a subordinate place: it had held out the hope of immortality. But only a select number could pretend to follow the philosophical arguments on which these beliefs rested. No authority, except the authority of philosophers, could be alleged in their behalf. The nature-worship of polytheism gave no real support to the ethical monotheism of the philosophers. The Christians on the other hand found the ultimate basis of their teaching in an historical revelation. The God whom they worshipped, was a God who had made Himself

[1] A compromise between pure Monotheism and popular Monotheism seems to have been generally accepted throughout the empire in the latter part of the second century. Maximus the Syrian, a rhetorician who lived in the time of the Antonines, says (*Diss.* xvii. 5) that most people, whether Greeks or barbarians, educated or uneducated, believed that there was one God, the king and father of, all, the other gods being his children and coadjutors. Eusebius (*Laud. Constantin.* 1) gives a similar account of the general sentiment and takes advantage of it in the interests of Christianity.

known. The philosophers spoke at best of a God whom they had found, the Christians of a God who had found them. He had been with Adam and the Patriarchs, he had made Himself known by name to Moses. He had chosen and directed the Hebrew people, He had spoken through the prophets and declared His holy will. Last of all He had revealed Himself in Jesus, had sealed Christ's teaching by miracles, and given assurance of immortality with its attendant rewards and punishments by raising him from the dead. It is true that this method of proof does not satisfy many of us as it did satisfy the men of the third century. It may be objected, and justly, that the early Christians who had such contempt for the mythology of the Greeks, were advancing myths of their own. Nevertheless, the difference between the position of heathen philosophers and Christians with respect to revelation was immense. The Greek myths are natural, and contain little morality. The Hebrew myths in the oldest form accessible to us have in nearly every case been deeply coloured by the ethical religion of the prophets, and have become the vehicles of moral instruction.

(3) Again, the history of revelation, from which the Christians drew their authority, was far from being purely mythical. It was undeniable that one prophet after another had professed to speak by divine inspiration, that the Jews were the single instance of a monotheistic nation, that they had reached a level of religious development which gave them from the religious point of view an incomparable superiority to the more cultivated nations who ruled over them. The grandest utterances of Stoic or Neoplatonist philosophers did not touch the heart like many an oracle of the prophets, many a passionate cry

and devout aspiration of the psalmists. Above all, the divine life had really manifested itself in the real man Jesus. Let men think as they would of his miracles and resurrection (and the reader cannot be too often reminded that the canons of historical criticism were much laxer in the third century than in the nineteenth), at least his trust and hope, the love to God and man which penetrated his whole being, were in the strictest sense historical. We may feel constrained to dismiss the accounts of his apparition after death, but no criticism can alter the fact that he was crucified, and, 'being lifted up from the earth' was 'drawing all men to himself.'

(4) An historical religion, a religion which could exhibit its utmost ideal realised in human form—that was the want of the time, and the philosophers themselves became conscious of the need, and strove to meet it. They mingled philosophy with religion, and endeavoured to find authority for both in the ancient worships of the east, but they did not stop there. A remarkable work appeared in the early part of the third century. This was the life of Apollonius of Tyana, a famous magician who was a contemporary of Domitian. The life, written by the Neopythagorean philosopher Philostratus, is really not a biography but a romance. Apollonius is an historical name, but in the hands of Philostratus he becomes an imaginary character, the ideal of that mixture of philosophy and religion which was in favour with Julia Domna, wife of the Emperor Septimius Severus. Apollonius is possessed of consummate knowledge of philosophy, he is the pattern of a rigorously ascetic life, all the virtues are perfectly blended in his noble character, he has the gifts of prophecy and miracles.

But he is no recluse : he is not even a Stoic philosopher who trains a band of disciples, and leaves the crowd to their madness. He is a great religious reformer. He wanders from place to place, and especially from temple to temple. He despises death, and his love to mankind fires him with the one desire to awaken the slumbering forces of religion and morality, and recall men to the perfect offering of a pious and virtuous life. The resemblance to the life of Jesus cannot be mistaken, though of course it is a resemblance with important differences. Very likely Philostratus, the author of this romance, had no bitter hostility to the Christian religion. His object may have been to show that the light which shone in Jesus, displayed itself elsewhere also, that philosophy, too, had produced its ideal life. Yet what a confession of weakness, what a change of front does this imply! For the well-bred contempt of Lucian and Celsus we have the imitation of Christianity by Philostratus, an imitation which showed that he knew, more or less imperfectly, the real well-spring of Christian strength.

§ 3. The Power of Christianity over the Heart.

(1) For the Christian religion was a religion of power. Attempts are often made to question its originality. In our own day, learned Jews have tried to produce a parallel to each maxim of Jesus from the traditional sayings of Jewish Rabbis embalmed in the Talmud. From the other side (and this is the point which concerns us here), another set of parallels has been gathered from the Stoic philosphers. It is right that this work

should be done, though instances given require careful sifting, and a resemblance in words may often be mistaken for a resemblance in thought. But the originality, or the want of it, in the precepts, is not the chief question. If in these precepts there were no originality at all, we should still stand face to face with the fact that whereas philosophy did but strengthen the moral resolutions of small circles, and cause a few ameliorations in Roman law, Christianity changed the lives of multitudes. The reason is that the abstract God of philosophy could only with great difficulty and in a few men became an object of love. They might be resigned to the government of the Stoic God: they could hardly regard him as an ever-present Friend. But they could love the God and Father revealed in Christ. It is not too much to say that the fruitfulness of Stoic morality is due in great measure to the strange fortune which grafted it into the Christian church.

(2) The power which the gospel exercised over the heart, and its character as a revealed religion, made the Christian church possible. The actual form which the Catholic church took, was not Christian, but Roman. But it must be remembered that the church in apostolic times had a very remarkable unity of its own, before the Catholic federation of bishops had been so much as dreamt of. Nor could Catholic unity have arisen, had not the bishops been able to avail themselves of another and a nobler unity which already existed, and which was, not indeed without serious detriment, preserved beneath the Catholic organisation. This nobler unity depended on the power which the Christian religion had of providing a common faith, in which men of all nations, of all social

ranks, of all grades in intellect and education, could meet together. Philosophy, even the Neoplatonist philosophy with its tincture of religion and theosophy, utterly failed to found a church. How could it? Philosophy is not for all, but only for intellectual persons with time at their command. Now Christianity provided matter for the deepest reflection. It enlisted the best philosophy of the day upon its side. At the same time it spoke of facts which were intelligible to the simplest. Rich and poor could believe in the same God and Father, could learn the lessons taught by the life of Jesus, and accept the gospel of divine communion and eternal hope. Christians acknowledged one master under God, one leader and perfect example, and the life which all prized, and which made them all one, was no fiction like that of Apollonius, but a life which was in its essential features historical and real. Thus in an age which was fond of associations, Christianity supplied an association which was world-wide, and compared with which all other associations were insignificant. The brotherhood of man, which was a theory with the Stoics, had become practical. The union of the Jews was the only one which could rival the Christian union, and Judaism suffered from the incurable defects of nationalism and exclusiveness. When Julian headed the heathen reaction against Christianity, he paid the new religion the compliment of imitating its organisation. He might have reproduced the episcopal organisation easily enough, but heathen religion and heathen philosophy lacked that unity of belief and of desire, failing which all outward organisation is useless.

(3) If, moreover, Christianity gathered men of all

classes into its net, it had a special message for the poor, for the outcast and the slave. It is the religion which consecrates sorrow, it is the religion of a crucified master, it is the religion of active benevolence. Its first success was won among the poor and the wretched. Its ultimate success was secured in the main by the same means, because the poor were becoming more and more the overwhelming majority in the Empire. The confiscation of large estates without encouragement of small proprietors, the accumulation of capital in a few hands, the absence of the economical conditions which produce wealth, intestine wars, the incursion of barbarians, combined to swell the mass of pauperism. These causes did not operate to their full extent till after the age of the Antonines, but pauperism before their time had assumed alarming proportions, and Trajan had to make provision for pauper children one of the public burdens. Christianity gave the sympathy for which the wretched crave. If it did not for the time make formal objection to slavery, it reminded the master that he too had a master in heaven. Master and slave prayed together, ate together at the love-feast, died together for the Christian name. The poor were rich in faith, and believed that their sufferings would disappear in the glory which was to be revealed. Meantime the church was a vast charitable institution which succoured the poor and the wretched in their present need. The Roman church in the middle of the third century supported fifteen hundred widows and other indigent persons, and sent help to brethren in the far east in Syria and Arabia. Within a few days Cyprian was able to collect a large sum among the Christians of Carthage for the redemption of Christian captives. This

charity was exercised in the first place in the household
of the faith, but it overflowed the bounds of the church
and reached the heathen population. We can but too
easily understand the social strain of the Roman Empire.
But only by a strong effort of imagination can we appreciate the effect of a brotherly love which was a new
creation.

§ 4. Limitations to the Efficacy of Christianity.

(1) There was a darker side to the picture. In the
apostolic age, Christian communities were stained by the
vices of the world around them, and to these they added
a controversial rancour which was their own. The
Catholic church fell far below the religious and moral
level of apostolic times, and the history of the church in
the early centuries is a history of increasing worldliness.
In the first three centuries, the progress of corruption
was arrested by the dangers of persecution, which might
break out at any moment, and which afforded a certain
test of Christian sincerity. Nevertheless, even then, signs
of moral decay were not wanting, and the episcopal
power was of itself an incentive to ambition. The
toleration granted to the church revealed the effect of
the deterioration which had taken place, by giving free
play to the forces which had long been working within
the church. Men were often disposed to regard strict
virtue as the business of monks. They led easy lives,
took their pleasure in the feasts of Christian martyrs, as
their fathers had done in the feasts of the gods, and
trusted in amulets and the intercession of the saints with

a devotion which was little better than heathenism. In the fever of metaphysical dispute which spread like a plague over the eastern half of the Empire, the interests of the Christian life fared badly, and an orthodox divine of the fifth century confesses that many acted as if Christ had only left directions about dogma and been altogether silent about moral conduct. There are, however, three considerations which should be taken into account, and which ought to modify the severity of our judgment.

(2) In the first place, when we would judge the morality of the Catholic church at the end of the third century, we may test it by one or other of two standards. We may compare its morality with the morality of the Sermon on the Mount, and be at no loss to discover the base metal with which the pure gold has been alloyed. Or, on the other hand, we may compare Christian morality with the morality current in the rest of the Empire. In that case our estimate will be very different. The Empire under Diocletian could make little claim to the patriotism and public spirit which shone forth in the palmy days of Athens and of Rome. In the purity of family life, in all private virtue, the Christians were far ahead of their fellow citizens. A Christian bishop was very unlike an apostle: but his office was in some ways very like that of a Roman magistrate, and it would be an extravagant scepticism to doubt that the bulk of the bishops were better men than the average of Imperial officials. It could not well be otherwise. A bishop might be chosen and enter on his office, knowing that he might be called to face the brunt of persecution. He was elected by the vote of the people, and the judgment of the other bishops in the province. Watchful eyes were upon him,

and he could not live an immoral life without giving scandal. He was expected to care for the poor. Paul of Samosata was charged by his adversaries with leading an immoral life. Whether the charges were true or false, they are at all events proof that immorality on the part of a bishop was considered to be disreputable and monstrous, whereas in the case of a Roman magistrate, nobody would have thought such matters worth notice. Further it as least certain that Christianity, when it became the religion of the state, did expel the most hideous forms of cruelty and of immorality. Now it is this latter standard of comparison which must be applied, when we inquire into the causes which made Christianity the religion of the Empire.

(3) Secondly, the bad effects of dogmatic controversy told much more severely on the bishops and theologians than upon ordinary Christians. Dogma avenged itself chiefly on those who busied themselves in its construction. The unlettered had more time to think of practical Christianity, and were far less likely to confuse religion with right opinion on the inscrutable problems of metaphysics. The layman might accept dogma with passive acquiescence. But he did not live in it or on it. Some exception must be made for the popularity of dogmatic dispute in the eastern church. But the western mind was more practical, and when Constantine became the patron of the church, speculative theology had only for a brief space intruded itself into the creed even of the eastern churches.

(4) Thirdly, the Catholic church qualified the mischief of its dogmas by its creation of the New Testament. A mass of old Christian literature has perished, and even

the works of the early and pre-Catholic writers which still survive, have been all but lost. They have only been preserved in one or two MSS. They were no longer suited to the taste of the age: they ceased to be read and were no longer copied: the old copies perished of neglect. It needs no great effort of imagination to see that the same fate might have overtaken the four gospels and the epistles of St. Paul. But the Catholic church took a middle course between the mere conservatism of Christians who simply held to the Old Testament, to the traditional sayings of Jesus, and to the utterances of Christian prophets, and the radicalism of the Gnostics, who were turning Christianity into systems of philosophic speculation. The rulers of the church promoted speculation, but they set limits to it by selecting the writings which form our New Testament, and by making a belief in their final and absolute authority an essential part of the Catholic system. The New Testament became a necessary part in the furniture of every church. Theologians commented on it. It was a repertory in which discordant divines sought and found texts for the support of their favourite doctrines, and the church zealously promoted the reading of the New Testament by the laity. Hence copies were multiplied, and so many survive, that the textual critic of to-day is perplexed by the abundance of his material. The most precious monuments of early Christianity were saved from destruction. For the time, for a long time, the church triumphed by the consummate skill which enabled it thus to mingle the old with the new. Yet the church, and we can never be too thankful that it was so, unwittingly preserved a witness which could testify against the corruptions which were setting in. In after ages, the corruptions became so great that the contrast could no longer be ignored, and the later Catholic church was fain to silence the witness which the earlier Catholic church had preserved. The voice of that witness has still much to say, more than any of us can foretell. At the Reformation, justice was done to the theology, and even perhaps to the religion, of St. Paul. Can we say that justice has been done to the religion of Jesus? Christianity, said Lessing, has existed for many centuries: the religion of Christ still remains to be tried.

# APPENDIX A.

## TABLE OF ROMAN EMPERORS.

A.D.

| | |
|---|---|
| 14 | Death of Octavianus Augustus. |
| 14—37 | Tiberius. |
| 37—41 | Caius Cæsar (Caligula). |
| 41—54 | Claudius. |
| 54—68 | Nero. |
| 68—69 | Galba. |
| 69 | Otho. Vitellius. |
| 69—79 | Vespasian. |
| 79—81 | Titus. |
| 81—96 | Domitian. |
| 96—98 | Nerva. |
| 98—117 | Trajan. |
| 117—138 | Hadrian. |
| 138—161 | Antoninus Pius. |
| 161—180 | Marcus Antoninus (Marcus Aurelius). |
| 180—193 | Commodus. |
| 193 | Pertinax. Didius Salvius Julianus. |

## APPENDIX A

| A.D. | |
|---|---|
| 193—211 | Septimius Severus. |
| 211—217 | Antoninus Bassianus Caracalla. |
| 217—218 | Macrinus. |
| 218—222 | Elagabalus. |
| 222—235 | Severus Alexander. |
| 235—238 | Maximinus Thrax. |
| 238—244 | Gordianus. |
| 244—249 | Philippus (Philip the Arab). |
| 249—251 | Decius. |
| 251—283 | Gallus. |
| 253—268 | Valerian and Gallienus. |
| 268—270 | Claudius. |
| 270—275 | Aurelian. |
| 275—276 | Claudius Tacitus. |
| 276—282 | Probus. |
| 282—284 | Carus. Carinus. Numerianus. |
| 284—305 | Diocletian. He in 285 nominates Maximian co-emperor. In 292 Constantius and Galerius are raised to the dignity of Cæsars. |
| 305 | Diocletian and Maximian abdicate. Constantius and Galerius Emperors. Maximin Daza and Severus become Cæsars. |
| 306 | Death of Constantius. Severus becomes Emperor; Constantine Cæsar. Maxentius is proclaimed Emperor, and his father Maximian resumes the purple. |
| 307 | Death of Severus. He is succeeded by Licinius. Constantine declares himself Emperor. So does Maximin in Asia. |

| A.D. | |
|---|---|
| 310 | Maximian forced to kill himself at Marseilles. |
| 311 | Galerius dies. |
| 312 | Maxentius defeated at the Ponte Molle and drowned in the Tiber. |
| 313 | Defeat and death of Maximin. Constantine and Licinius sole Emperors. |
| 314 | War between Constantine and Licinius. |
| 323 | Second War between Constantine and Licinius. |
| 324 | Licinius slain. |
| 324—337 | Constantine sole Emperor. |

# APPENDIX B.

## CHIEF POINTS IN THE CHURCH HISTORY OF THE FIRST THREE CENTURIES.

### FIRST PERIOD.

From the death of Jesus in 31 A.D. (?) till the accession of Trajan in 98.

*Characteristics.*

According to a tradition ancient, general, and still accepted by many scholars, one Apostle, viz., John, survived till about the end of this period, and in any case the main features of the Apostolic age were preserved throughout. There was no persecution of Christians as such by the Roman power. The churches recognised no bond of union except common trust, hope, and sanctity of life. The Church was governed by 'the Spirit'; instruction was in the hands of wandering Apostles and Prophets, and of teachers with supernatural gifts. The separate churches had no organization, no officials, except that in most churches, perhaps in all towards the close of the period, a board of overseers

## SECOND PERIOD

*Note the following events.*

112. Trajan declares the Christian religion illegal. Persecution of Christians in Bithynia under Pliny.

115 (?). Martyrdom of Ignatius of Antioch.

125. Quadratus and Aristides (according to Eusebius; see, however, p. 107, above) present apologies for the Christian religion to Hadrian.

132-135. Revolt of Palestinian Jews under Barcochba. Ælia Capitolina, a heathen city, is built on the site of Jerusalem.

140. Valentinus the Gnostic leaves Alexandria and takes up his abode in Rome.

140-155. Marcion at Rome.

147-160. Between these years Justin's two Apologies were written. His Dialogue with the Jew Trypho a little later.

150-1. Shortly after this time Montanus began to prophesy in Phrygia, and starts a movement which spreads through the Christian world.

165. Martyrdom of Justin. Then also, or according to another calculation ten years before, the martyrdom of Polycarp.

177. Martyrs of Vienne and Lyons. In the same year Athenagoras addresses his *Supplication for the Christians* to M. Aurelius.

178. About this year Celsus writes his *True Discourse* against Christianity.

180. Theophilus of Antioch publishes his three books *To Autolycus*. First known use of the word Trinity (in the Greek form 'trias"), and first formal quotation from St. John's Gospel.

P

## APPENDIX B

### THIRD PERIOD.

From the consolidation of the Catholic Church towards the close of the second century to the reunion of the Empire under Constantine in 324.

### *Characteristics.*

During this period the old union of religious trust and brotherly love is finally replaced by the Catholic Church, *i.e.*, by a world-wide organisation subject to an aristocratic federation of bishops. The bishops, therefore, are no longer mere presidents of particular congregations, but officials of the church at large and successors of the Apostles, charged with the duty of delivering and maintaining the 'rule of faith.' They are the defenders of the common faith against Gnostic heresy. They are the official teachers. They guarantee the 'canon,' or list of New Testament books, which are authoritative and inspired. Thus 'prophecy' as an abiding gift falls into discredit or is confined within narrow bounds, inspiration being now chiefly a thing of the past. Theological speculation, restrained by the 'rule of faith,' flourishes in the east, and its results begin to find a place in the formal creeds of the eastern churches. The hostility of the empire to the church, becomes more resolute and systematic. On the other hand, the church looks forward to the conversion of the empire. Hence the hope of Christ's speedy return to establish the Kingdom of God upon earth grows dim and in some quarters fades away altogether. The church, adapting itself to the world, relaxes her moral discipline. The controversies within the church turned chiefly on the Person of Christ and his relations to the Father, the treatment of the 'lapsed' (*i.e.* those who had betrayed the faith under persecution), and the validity of baptism by heretics.

*Note the following events.*

190 or thereabouts, Irenæus, bishop of Lyons, finishes his *Refutation and Overthrow of Gnosticism falsely so called.*

190-200 (?). Victor, bishop of Rome. He excommunicates Theodotus, who held that Jesus was a 'mere man.'

193-211. Septimius Severus Emperor. Persecution of the Christians.

200(?)-223. Zephyrinus and then Callistus bishops of Rome. Literary activity of Hippolytus, the Roman presbyter. He contends against the Roman bishops, making himself the champion of strict discipline and of the doctrine that the Logos or Word is distinct from and subordinate to the Father. About this time the doctrine that Christ is absolutely identical with the Father is maintained at Rome by Sabellius and others, finds favour for a time with the Roman bishops, and enjoys a wide popularity till after the middle of the third century.

220. Death of Tertullian who is about 60 years of age, and of Clement of Alexandria.

241. Ammonius Saccas, founder of Neoplatonism and teacher of Origen, dies.

244-249. Within this time Origen completes his great work *Against Celsus.*

249-258. Cyprian bishop of Carthage.

250. Persecution under Decius. It is renewed by Valerian 253-260.

**251.** Cornelius bishop of Rome. Novatian leads a party which refuses to admit repentant sinners, guilty of idolatry and other great crimes. The schism begins at Rome and extends throughout the church.

**253-257** (?). Stephen bishop of Rome. He admits the validity of baptism by heretics, if given in due form. He is resisted by Cyprian of Carthage, Firmilian of Cæsarea, and others. The Roman practice, despite its novelty, finally prevails at the beginning of the fourth century.

**261.** Gallienus stays the persecution. The church left in peace during forty years.

**268-269.** Paul of Samosata, the bishop of Antioch, is excommunicated for holding that Christ is one with God in will but not in essence. Final triumph of the Logos doctrine.

**303.** Persecution of Diocletian begins.

**313.** Edict of Milan makes Christianity a lawful religion.

**324.** Constantine already a Christian, though not yet baptised, becomes sole Emperor.

# APPENDIX C.

## 1. HEATHEN WRITERS.

We have brief references to Christianity in TACITUS, who was a child of eight or ten when Nero persecuted the Christians in 64. He was a magistrate under Domitian and wrote his most important works under Trajan. SUETONIUS, who makes an obscure allusion to Christ in his *Lives of the Twelve Cæsars*, was a younger contemporary of Tacitus. He was secretary to the Emperor Hadrian. The correspondence between PLINY the younger and TRAJAN about the Christians belongs to the year 112.

We have also references to the Christians in GALEN, a famous authority on medicine and logic, who wrote about 160, and in the Meditations of M. AURELIUS (about 174). LUCIAN, who was a Syrian by birth, but wrote in elegant Greek, ridicules the Christians in a book on the *Death of Peregrinus*, written shortly after 165.

The best known controversial writers against Christianity were CELSUS (about 178), PORPHYRY the Neoplatonist (about 270), and HIEROCLES, who took an active part in the persecution under Galerius, and wrote about 303. All these anti-Christian books have perished and are only known to us by the fragments preserved in the Christian answers to them.

## 2. CHRISTIAN LITERATURE.

(1) THE APOSTOLIC FATHERS.

The name implies that the authors were in some special way connected with the Apostles, generally as their disciples. The title is justified only so far as this, that the writings of the Apostolic Fathers present a very early and simple form of Christianity, little influenced by philosophical theory. These writings comprise:

*Two Epistles ascribed to Clement.* Who this Clement was is quite uncertain. The former epistle was addressed by the Church of Rome to the Church at Corinth, then agitated by discontent with its presbyters, and disputes about the management of the flock. The epistle was written about 98 and CLEMENT may have been a Roman presbyter who had the chief hand in its composition. The second so-called epistle is the most ancient Christian sermon extant. The place of its origin and date are uncertain. It may well belong to the earliest half of the second century.

The *Shepherd of Hermas:* an exhortation to penance in the form of visions and prophecies. According to a very old tradition, the author, HERMAS, was the brother of Pius, who was said to have been bishop of Rome about the middle of the second century.

*The Epistle of Barnabas.* A treatise on the typical sense of the Jewish ceremonial law, followed by a moral discourse on 'the Two Ways' of life and death. It can scarcely be later than the early part of Hadrian's reign (117), but is probably a compilation of two documents.

Closely connected with the epistle of Barnabas is the recently discovered *Didachê* or *Teaching of the Apostles*. It consists of moral precepts under the heading of 'the Two Ways' and of rules for the worship and discipline of the Christian Churches. It belongs to a transition period, when the old enthusiasm was giving way to the government of officials, though monarchical episcopacy had not yet arisen. Little more is certain, in the present division of opinion on the date of the book and the documents of which it is composed.

*The Ignatian Epistles.* It is said that IGNATIUS, bishop of Antioch, was condemned to death under Trajan, that he was transported to Rome, and died there a martyr's death in the Amphitheatre. A number of letters which bear his name profess to have been written by him on his journey. Their authenticity has been the subject of controversy which has lasted for three centuries and still continues. They have come down to us in three recensions differing from one another in extent, number, and character. Now, however, the question is practically limited to seven *epistles* in the 'Shorter Greek Recension' known to Eusebius. These are addressed to the Churches of Ephesus, Magnesia, Tralles, Rome, Philadelphia, Smyrna, and to Polycarp. They denounce Judaism and the Docetic doctrine that Christ only 'seemed' to be a man. They insist on submission to the bishop, who represents Christ, and to the presbyters, who take the place of the Apostles. Those who deny the authenticity of the epistles, admit that they must have been written as early as 150. Those who contend for their authenticity, place them at various dates from the first decade of the second century to about 130. On any theory, they supply evidence of great moment for the rise of the monarchical episcopate in the Churches of Syria and Asia Minor.

POLYCARP. We have an *Epistle* under his name to the Philippians, parts of which only survive in a Latin version. Polycarp is said to have been bishop of Smyrna and disciple of St. John. The authenticity of the epistle stands or falls with that of the Ignatian epistles. If genuine and free from interpolation, it must have been written about the same time.

PAPIAS, bishop of Hierapolis in Phrygia, wrote five books entitled an *Exposition of the Oracles of the Lord*. Of this work a few fragments remain which give valuable information on the origin of Mark's Gospel, and the collection of discourses by Jesus which Matthew compiled in Hebrew or Aramaic; they also contain fantastic accounts of the Millennium and a fabulous story about the death of Judas. Papias was a sedulous collector of oral tradition from the mouths of those who had conversed with the Apostles. His date is uncertain, but he collected the sayings of men who had known the Apostles.

HEGESIPPUS, a Christian of Jewish origin, visited European Churches, notably Corinth and Rome, and lived till about 189. His *Memoirs* in five books seem to have been a protest against doctrinal novelties on the historical ground of apostolic tradition.

An anonymous *Epistle to Diognetus* is usually printed among the works of the 'Apostolic Fathers.' But it is much more akin to the works of the Apologists. The date is quite uncertain, nor is it known who or what Diognetus was.

We have also a contemporary account of the *Martyrdoms at Vienne* and Lyons in 177; and another of *Polycarp's Martyrdom* in 165 (?), which professes to come from the members of the Church at Smyrna who witnessed it. It is probably genuine in substance, though this has been doubted.

(2) THE GNOSTIC WRITERS.

(3) THE APOLOGISTS OF THE SECOND CENTURY.

A sketch of the history with the names and dates of the chief Gnostic writers and apologists has been given above, chaps. iv. and vi. Of the Gnostic literature scarcely anything survives, except fragments preserved in the writings of their Catholic opponents. The only Gnostic book handed down to us entire, has survived in a Coptic translation. It is called *Pistis-Sophia*, and was written by a disciple of the Gnostic Valentinian in the third century. Some of the Apocryphal Gospels are coloured by Gnostic tendencies.

(4) THE FATHERS OF THE OLD CATHOLIC CHURCH, TILL THE REIGN OF CONSTANTINE.

(*a*) *The School of Asia Minor and Rome.*

IRENÆUS, knew Polycarp in his youth; went to Lyons, where he was presbyter, and after 177 or 178 bishop. His great work, *Refutation and Overthrow of Gnosticism falsely so called*, has been preserved chiefly in a Latin translation. This version, generally supposed to be nearly contemporaneous with the original Greek, belongs according to Westcott and Hort to the fourth century (see their edition of the New Testament, vol. ii. p. 160). Irenæus, though a strenuous advocate of the Catholic system, keeps something of the older and simpler religion. He opposed extreme measures against the Montanists, and withstood the attempt of the Roman bishop to enforce uniformity in the observance of Easter.

HIPPOLYTUS, a disciple of Irenæus. He was presbyter at Rome in the first two or three decades of the second century. He defended the sharp distinction between the Logos or Word and the supreme God, and was the champion of strict discipline against the Roman bishops of his day. For a time he presided over a Schismatical Church at Rome. He was a man of great learning and a prolific writer, though most of his works have perished. His more important extant work is his 'Refutation of all Heresies.' It was printed for the first time in 1851 as the *Philosophumena* of Origen, and is still usually quoted under that title.

(*b*) *The Latin Fathers.*

TERTULLIAN (160-220). Born at Carthage, studied law and rhetoric, wrote at first in Greek, then in Latin, though none of his Greek works remain. His extant works, which are numerous, are partly defences of Christianity in general, partly attacks on heresy, especially those of the Gnostics and Sabellians; in a third class he discusses morals and discipline. He was a passionate advocate of the Catholic system, but equally passionate in maintenance of strict discipline, and his moral works exhibit his gradual passage from the Catholic Church to the extreme rigorism of the Montanists. Tertullian is the father of ecclesiastical Latinity and to a great extent of Latin theology. MINUCIUS FELIX may have written Latin earlier. But it was Tertullian, not Minucius Felix, who first gave a definite character to the Latin of the Church.

CYPRIAN, who used to call Tertullian his 'Master,' and studied him diligently, was bishop of Carthage,

248-259. He was no theologian, but did much to build up the episcopal system of the Church. His chief works are *On the Unity of the Church, On Work and Alms, On the Lapsed* (*i.e.* those who had fallen into idolatry, etc.), besides many *Letters*, which throw a flood of light on the constitution and internal life of the Church.

LACTANTIUS. (Lucius Cœlius or Cæcilius Lactantius Firmianus). A rhetorician at Nicomedia under Diocletian. He became a Christian and laid down his office during the persecution. Afterwards he was tutor to Crispus, son of Constantine, and died about 330. Besides the seven books of *Divine Institutions* (*i.e.* of instructions in the divine or Christian religion), a treatise on the *Deaths of Persecutors* is probably his.

(*c*) *The Alexandrian School.*

CLEMENT of Alexandria (Titus Flavius Clemens), a man of philosophic education who travelled and studied in many lands, being specially attracted by Platonism and by the moral teaching of the Stoics. He became a Christian, and settled at Alexandria, where he presided over the Catechetical School. He died about 220. His chief extant works are an *Apology for Christianity*, a treatise on Christian asceticism (called Pædagogus) and seven books of *Stromaties*, *i.e.* patchwork, or Miscellanies, which treat, but without system, of the Christian religion from a philosophic point of view.

ORIGEN. Born of Christian parents at Alexandria. Studied under Clement and also under Ammonius Saccas the Neoplatonist. Travelled to Rome, where he met Hippolytus, and to Antioch, where (at her own request) he met the mother of the Emperor Alexander Severus. He was asked to preach, and then in 230 ordained presbyter, by the bishops of Jerusalem and Caesarea in Palestine. This bitterly offended Demetrius the bishop of Alexandria, who had not been consulted in the matter. Therefore Origen left Alexandria and established a theological School at Caesarea. He died under Valerian in 254.

Origen knew nearly all that could be known in his day, and, more than that, is the true founder of Greek Christian theology. From him, as from a centre all subsequent developments radiate, sometimes in directions contrary to each other. His numerous works fall chiefly into three classes. In his *Hexapla*, Origen placed the Hebrew text of the Old Testament, and four Great Versions, in parallel columns, specially marking the relations of the Septuagint text to the Hebrew. He also wrote homilies and commentaries on the books of the Bible. Some of these exegetical works survive in Greek, many more in a Latin translation. Next in his book *On Principles* Origen supplied the first example of dogmatic speculation, reduced to system. This work belongs to the Alexandrian or early period of Origen's activity. It only survives, as a whole, in a Latin version which is not always to be trusted. Thirdly, in his eight books *Against Celsus*, Origen wrote towards the end of his career the most powerful defence of Christianity known to the ancient world.

The bishop of Alexandria who opposed Origen was succeeded in 232 or 233 by Heraclas, and he by the celebrated Dionysius who died in 264. Both were disciples of Origen, and the theological School of Alexandria closely adhered to the lines laid down by the great teacher till the close of the third century.

GREGORY the wonder-worker (Thaumaturgus) was a pupil of Origen in Palestine. He died bishop of Neocæsarea in Pontus, in 270. He has left a *Panegyric* on Origen and an *Exposition* of the faith in his Master's spirit.

EUSEBIUS, 265-340, bishop of Cæsarea in Palestine, was the disciple of Pamphilus the disciple of Origen, and was the chief heir of Origen's learning and theological principles. His *history of the Church* from the beginning to 324 has a unique value, because of the numerous extracts which it gives from early Aristean works and documents, otherwise inaccessible to us. In his *Chronicles*, he gave a sketch of the history of the world with chronological tables. His *Life of Constantine* is written in the spirit of a courtier rather than of an historian. Farther, Eusebius devoted himself to the interpretation of scripture; he superintended the preparation of fifty copies of the Greek Bible for the Church of Constantinople; he is the author of works in defence of Christianity against the Heathen (*Preparation for the Gospel*), and against the Jews (*Demonstration of the Gospel*). He also wrote books in theology proper, but these last are connected with the fourth, rather than with the first three centuries of Church history.

THE END.

# INDEX.

*Prepared by H. R. APPLETON.*

ABGAR 41, 42
Abraham 78
Acts of the Apostles 64, 106
Addai 41
Adoption, under Empire 9
Ælia Capitolina 38
Aeschines 188
Africa 45, 46, 60, 76
Agrippinus 45
Alexander, of Abonoteichos 13
Alexander, of Ephesus 65
Alexander Severus 51, 75
Alexandria 30, 38, 41, 44, 79, 143, 163, 219
Alogoi 174
Ammonius Saccas 26
Annona 16
Antioch 12, 30, 36, 37, 38, 41, 65, 79, 163
Antonines 13, 20, 25, 149, 188, 197
Antoninus Pius 32, 71, 72
Apocalypse 43, 68
Apologists, The 105, 120, 122, 124, 127, 142, 144, 146, 149, 173, 217.
Apostolic Fathers 105, 214
Apostolic Succession 163, 166
Apostles, The 39, 43, 49, 95, 96, 141, 152, 157, 163, 164, 169, 172, 191, 195, 198, 215
Appolonius 193, 196
Aquileia 45
Aquinas Thomas 136
Arabs 42
Areopagus 106
Aristides 107, 108, 109
Aristotle and Aristotelianism 21, 25, 149
Arles 45, 47, 48
Armenia 42, 43
Army, Roman 7, 75
Arval Brothers 15
Ascetics and Asceticism 137, 187
Asia Minor 38, 43
Athanasius 91, 191

Atheism and Atheists 40, 55, 73, 115, 116
Athenagoras 110, 120
Athens 37, 44
Augurs and Auguries 15
Augustine 64
Augustus 3, 4, 6, 7, 9, 13, 30, 86
Aurelian 84, 176

BAPTISM 136, 168, 173, 179, 180, 189
Barbarians 81, 107, 115, 116, 120, 197
Barberini 180
Barca 44
Barnabas 135, 214
Basilides 149, 153
Benedict 186
Berenice 32
Berkeley 26
Bible, The 46, 103, 170
Bishops 40, 161, 164, 188, 195, 199
Bithynia 43, 51, 69
Britain 4, 48
British India 3

CÆCILIUS 57
Cærleon 48
Cæsarea 36
Caligula 32
Callistus 166, 182
Canius Julius 20
Canon, The 158, 171
Capua 45
Caracalla 10, 77
Carthage 45, 85.
Catacombs 52
Catherine 107
Catholic Church 94, 105, 109, 119, 125, 126, 134, 137, 138, 145, 146, 159, 160, 164, 178, 182, 187, 190, 195, 198, 200

# INDEX

Celsus 14, 51, 57, 123, 154, 194, 213
Censor 81
Centralisation of Government under Roman Empire 10
Cerinthus 148
Charity 197
China 4
Chrestos 65
Christ : see under Jesus Christ
Christianity 16-28, 35-40, 37, 50, 51, 53, 56, 58, 65, 90, 98, 115, 152, 168, 185, 191, 195, 202
Christus 65
Chrysippus 21
Church, The, and Churches 46, 49, 80, 88, 90, 94, 127, 145, 160, 162, 163, 191, 197, 201, 206
Cicero 13, 123
Citizenship (of Rome) 9, 10, 54, 58, 70, 74
Claudius 32, 65
Claudius Apollinaris 109
Clement 136, 189, 214, 219
Clubs 19, 59, 70, 77, 161
Colonies 5
Columella 11
Commentaries 153
Commerce 49
Commodus 9, 61, 71, 75
Communion 180
Constantine 57, 86, 87, 89, 90, 91, 92, 185, 186, 200
Constitution of Church 94
Convent of St. Catherine 107
Convoking Assembly of Roman People 6
Copts 44
Cordova 47
Corinth 12, 30, 37, 39, 44
Cornelius 44, 183
Creeds 95, 124, 127, 169, 191
Crete 44
Cynics and Cynicism 22
Cyprian 85, 164, 177, 181, 182, 197, 218
Cyprus 36, 37
Cyrenaica 44

DEACONS 161
Decius 8, 61, 64, 80, 81, 82
Defence, Learned, of Christianity 93
Deism 124
Democracy 5
Demosthenes 188
Despotism of Roman Empire 8
Didache 215
Dio Cassius 15, 51
Diocletian 10, 85, 86, 87, 88, 89, 199
Diognetus 216

Dionysius 44, 79, 138, 177
Disciples 36
Discipline 182
Dispensation, The 174
Dogma and Dogmatism 122, 127, 188, 191, 199, 200
Domitian 9, 40, 68, 69, 193
Domitilla 40

EARLY Church Government 161
Easter 166
Edessa 41, 42
Egypt 7, 8, 44, 76, 83
Elagabalus 62, 76, 77, 78
Elders 161
Eleusinian Mysteries 180
Elvira 47, 182
Emesa 77
Emperors, Roman 7, 9, 61, 69, 75, 76, 203
Encratites 138
Ephesus 12, 30, 38, 39, 65
Epictetus 20, 22, 24, 51, 57, 134
Epicurus and Epicureanism 21, 25, 56
Episcopacy : see under Bishops
Episkopoi 161
Epistles 35
Erastus 39
Essenes 137
Eucharist 180, 189
Eusebius 40, 44, 49, 75, 78, 79, 185, 221
Evangelists 49

FABIAN 183
Faith, Rule of 168, 173
Famines 12
Fathers, The 149, 214, 217, 218
Father of Fathers 18
Federation of Bishops 164, 188, 195
Flavius Clemens 40
Foreign Elements in Christianity 187
French Language 11
Fronto 74
Fructuosus 85

GAIUS 39
Galen 187, 213
Galerius 86, 87, 88, 89, 90
Gallienus 26, 84
Gallio 65
Gallus 82
Gaul 46, 47, 74
Geographical limits of Roman Empire 3
Germany 47

# INDEX

Gladiators 25
Gnostics and Gnosticism 138, 147, 162, 168, 173, 177, 178, 201, 217
Gospels 98
Goths 8, 81, 85
Greece and Greeks 5, 11, 14, 28, 38, 44, 46, 54, 96, 97, 98, 105, 107, 111, 113, 114, 115, 117, 131, 133, 141, 142, 144, 146, 168, 179, 187, 189
Gregory 42, 43, 221
Gregory, of Tours 47
Growth of Speculative Theology 173

HADRIAN 13, 17, 20, 25, 32, 38, 71, 72, 107
Heathens and Heathenism 12, 30, 50, 65, 86, 92, 119, 129, 136, 158, 196, 213
Hebrews and Hebraism 101, 102, 106, 112, 113, 114, 117, 119, 130, 145, 152, 170, 173
Hegesippus 68, 69, 216
Hellenism 105
Heracleon 153
Heraclitus 21, 115
Heresy and Heretics 103, 104, 183
Hermas 214
Herod 31, 37
Hierocles 213
High Treason 59
Hippolytus 218
History, Chief points of first three centuries of Church 206
Homer 103, 114
Homily 188
Horace 13, 33
Hume 26

IDOLATRY 116, 120
Ignatius 63, 163, 215
Incarnation 125
India 4
Influence of Greece on Christianity 96, 105
Influence of Religion 12
Intellectualism in Christianity 144, 147
Irenæus 46, 47, 48, 75, 142, 163, 166, 171, 217
Isis 17
Italy 44, 47

JACOB 118
Jerome 46, 107
Jerusalem 35, 36, 38
Jesus Christ 35, 37, 41, 50, 54, 68, 69, 78, 94, 97, 113, 114, 115, 117, 118, 120, 125, 130, 134, 140, 173, 185, 192, 194, 202
Jews, Judæa, and Judaism 12, 30, 31, 40, 56, 62, 65, 66, 67, 77, 78, 97, 99, 105, 106, 107, 111, 114, 118, 129, 137, 140, 152, 181, 194, 196
John 38, 68, 142, 143
Joppa 36
Josephus 33
Jude 68
Julia Domna 193
Julian 57, 188, 196
Julius Cæsar 30
Jurisprudence, Roman 10
Justin 73, 74, 108, 109, 113, 114, 125, 137, 141, 142, 170
Justinian 186

LACEDÆMON 44
Lactantius 219
Language, under Roman Empire 11
Latin 11, 111, 218
Legal Position of Christianity under Roman Empire 53
Leon 47, 61
Lessing 116, 202
Licinius 89, 90, 91
Literature 13, 28, 41, 46, 47, 54, 55, 71, 95, 131, 140, 145, 146, 189, 200, 213
Logos 102, 114, 119, 125
London 48
Lucan 11
Lucian 14, 194, 213
Lucretius 13
Luke 158
Luther, Martin 140
Lyons 46, 74

MACEDONIA 38
Macrianus 83
Madaura 74
Maecenas 13
Magic 56, 59, 62, 189
Magistrates 60, 64
Mahommed and Mahommedanism 42, 96
Malaga 47

## 226 INDEX

Malchion 176
Mammæa 78
Manichees 87
Marcia 62, 75
Marcion 157, 169
Marcus Aurelius 8, 13, 14, 22, 24, 44, 47, 51, 57, 61, 71, 73, 74, 75, 76, 108, 111, 116, 189, 213
Marcus 156
Mark 38
Marriage 138, 141
Martial 11
Martyrs 45, 63
Matthew 33
Mauretania 45, 61
Maxentius 89
Maximia Daza 89, 90, 186
Maximian 87, 89
Mayence 47
Melito 108
Merida 47
Messiah 35, 37, 106, 130, 131
Metaphysics 187, 191, 199
Milan 45, 64, 89, 90, 91
Millenium 142, 143
Minucius, Felix 111, 120, 121, 218
Miracles 192
Missionaries 49
Mithra 17, 18
Monachism 183
Monasticism 184, 197
Monotheism 17, 23, 129
Montanists 172, 182
Morality 133, 199
Moses 117, 118, 192
Moslems 189
Mount Palatine 56
Muratorian Canon 171
Musonius 22, 136
Mysteries 178, 189
Mythology 54

NATURE-WORSHIPS 54
Nazarenes 37, 65
Neander 159
Need of an Historical Religion 193
Neo-Cæsarea 44
Neoplatonism 26, 86, 149, 196
Nero 9, 66, 67, 68
Nerva 20, 69
New Testament 35, 44, 46, 105, 106, 132, 135, 145, 153, 170, 200, 201
Nicean Creed 191
Nicomedia 85
Novatian 183

OFFICERS of Early Church 162
Old Roman Worship 15, 16
Old Testament 98, 103, 137, 153, 170, 201
Ophites 148
Organisation of Catholic Church 127
Orientals as Senators and Emperors 7
Origen 1, 52, 78, 79, 80, 142, 150, 175, 177, 181, 187, 219
Originality of Christianity 190
Orpheus 78
Otho 14
Outcasts 197
Overseers 161

PÆDAGOGUS of Clement 136
Pagans and Paganism 51, 111
Palestine 38
Papias 141, 216
Papinian 8, 76
Paris 47
Parthia 4
Paul of Samosata 176, 177, 200
Paul 23, 29, 30, 38, 39, 43, 64, 65, 68, 95, 106, 107, 112, 132, 133, 137, 140, 141, 151, 157, 159, 168, 202
Paulus 8, 76
Pentateuch 112
Persia 4, 42, 85, 87
Persecutions 53, 63, 79, 85
Peter 38, 39, 45, 106
Pharisees 140
Philip, the Arab 62, 75, 79
Philippi 37, 65
Philo 99, 105, 106, 107, 114, 118
Philosophy 20, 52, 71, 92, 97, 99, 105, 106, 107, 108, 111, 113, 117, 119, 120, 124, 125, 129, 136, 149, 173, 177, 187, 192, 195, 196, 201
Philostratus 193
Phœnicia 36
Pirates 29
Pistis-Sophia 217
Plato and Platonism 21, 23, 25, 108, 118, 120, 149, 151
Pliny, the Elder 14
Pliny, the Younger 51, 57, 64, 69, 70, 71, 213
Plotinus 26, 27
Plutarch 17, 25, 113, 114
Polycarp 43, 72, 73, 216
Polytheism 16, 54, 116, 191
Pompey 37
Pontiffs 58
Pontus 43, 51, 69
Poor 197, 200

## INDEX

Poppæa 66
Porphyry 26, 27, 51, 213
Pothinus 46
Prætorians 7, 76
Prefecture 60
Presbyters and Presbyterianism 161
Priesthood 180, 184
Proconsuls 7
Protestant Churches 2
Psalms 46
Public rites 54, 56
Pythagoras and Pythagoreanism 14, 149

QUADRATUS 107, 108
Quintillian 11

REFORMATION, The 2, 202
Remus 166
Rennaissance 189
Republic, Roman 6, 7
Rise of Catholic Church 160
Roman Catholics 94, 172
Rome, Romans, and Roman Empire 3, 5, 8, 11, 28, 30, 38, 41, 44, 45, 46, 54, 58, 66, 75, 85, 131, 163, 165
Romulus 166
Rubellius Plautus 20
Rule of Faith 168, 173
Russian Empire 3

SABELLIUS and Sabellianism 175, 177
Sacraments 139
Sacrifices 13, 15
Sacrilege 59
Sahidic New Testament 44
Samaria and Samaritans 36, 147
Saragossa 47
Sardis 108
Saturninus 47
Scapula 45, 60
Scillis or Scillita 74
Scotch Philosophy 26
Scripture 130
Second coming of Jesus Christ 140
Secrecy of early Christian Assemblies 56
Senate and Senators of Rome 6, 7, 75, 81
Seneca 11, 22
Septimus Severus 44, 63, 75, 76, 77, 193

Serapis 17, 72
Sermon on the Mount 134, 199
Serpent-worshippers 148
Severa 79
Severus Alexander 62, 78, 79
Seville 47
Shepherd of Hermas 214
Sibyl 31
Sicily 45
Simon the Magician 147
Slaves and Slavery 5, 19, 25, 88, 141, 197
Smyrna 43, 72
Socrates 115, 116, 120
Sophists 110
Spain 11, 39, 47
Speculative Theology 173, 200
Stephen 35, 106
Stoics and Stoicism 21, 25, 27, 108, 113, 115, 149, 187, 189, 195, 196
Strabo 13
Strength of Christianity 190
Suetonius 40, 51, 65, 66, 213
Summa, The, of Thomas Aquinas 136
Sun God 17
Supernatural, The 15
Superstition 13
Synagogue, The 161
Syria 42

TABLE of Roman Emperors 203
Tacitus 14, 51, 66, 67, 213
Talmud 194
Tarragona 85
Tarsus 37
Tatian 110, 120, 121, 138
Taxation 8, 9
'Teaching of the Apostles,' The 49, 137, 215
Ten Tables 58
Terminus 88
Tertullian 4, 45, 46, 47, 48, 52, 56, 69, 76, 121, 166, 171, 174, 180, 218
Thebais 44
Theodosius 16
Theodotus 175
Theology and theologians 126, 127, 135, 173, 187, 200, 201, 202
Theophilus 120, 121, 126
Theosophy 27, 149
Thessalonica 37
Thrasea 20
Tiberias 9, 17
Tiridates 43
Titus 32, 38
Toledo 47

Toulouse 47
Tradition 146
Traditores 90
Trajan 4, 11, 20, 42, 51, 61, 63, 68, 69, 70, 71, 73, 74, 76, 77, 80, 81, 197, 213
Treves 47
Trinity, The 125, 126, 174
Trypho 110
Tuetons 4

ULPIAN 8, 76
Unity of Roman Empire 5
Unity of the Church 176
Universal Church 164

VALENTINIAN 149
Valerian 82
Vespasian 40
Victor 75, 166, 175
Vienne 46, 74

Virgil 13
Virginity 138
Virtue 134

WOMEN 19
Word, The 114, 117, 118, 120, 125, 126, 173, 174
Worship of Old Rome 15, 16
Worship of the genius of the Emperor 16, 59, 69, 77
Worship of the State 62
Writers, Christian 214
Writers, Heathen 213

YORK 48

ZENO 21
Zenobia 176
Zephyrinus 182
Zeus 24, 86

BIBLICAL MANUALS EDITED BY J. E. CARPENTER, M.A.

'They are among the first of their kind, and they meet a real want.'—
*Nineteenth Century.*

Life in Palestine when Jesus Lived. By Prof. J. E. Carpenter, M.A. Third edition. Cloth 1/-.
The Method of Creation. By Rev. H. W. Crosskey, LL.D. Second edition. Cloth 1/-.
Chapters on Job for Young Readers. By Rev. G. Vance Smith, D.D. Cloth 1/-.
Epistles to Philippians and Philemon. By Rev. V. D. Davis, B.A. Cloth 1/6.
Story of Jeremiah and his Times. By Harriet Johnson. Cloth 1/6.
Prophecies of the Captivity (Isaiah xl.-lxvi.). Ry Rev. R. T. Herford, B.A. Cloth 1/6.
The First Three Gospels: their Origin and Relations. By Prof. J. Estlin Carpenter, M.A. Cloth 3/6.
Epistle of Paul to the Galatians. By Principal Drummond, M.A., LL.D. Cloth 1/6.

Uniform with the above.

The Childhood of Jesus. By Rev. W. C. Gannett. Second edition. Cloth 1/6.

LESSON NOTES FOR TEACHERS.

Ten Lessons on Religion. By Rev. Charles Beard, LL.D. Price 1d.
Lessons for Little Boys. By Mary Dendy. Price 2d.
Lessons on the Growth of Moral and Spiritual Ideas. By Rev. P. H. Wicksteed, M.A. Price 4d.
Lessons on the Title Page and Table of Contents of an English Bible. By Rev. F. E. Millson. Limp cloth 8d.
In the Home: a Study of Duties. By Rev. W. C. Gannett. Price 3d.
Outline Lessons in Religion. By Rev. R. A. Armstrong, B.A. Price 6d.
Talks about the Sunday Services. By Rev. F. E. Millson. Price 3d.
The Three Stages of a Bible's Life. By Rev. W. C. Gannett. Sewed 4d., limp cloth 8d.

SUNDAY SCHOOL ASSOCIATION, ESSEX HALL, ESSEX ST., STRAND, LONDON, W.C.

www.ingramcontent.com/pod-product-compliance
Lightning Source LLC
Chambersburg PA
CBHW020805230426
43666CB00007B/865